Write Worlds Your Readers Won't Forget

A Second Toolkit for Emerging Writers

———————

Stant Litore

Westmarch Publishing

2017

MORE FROM STANT LITORE

PRAISE FOR *WRITE WORLDS YOUR READERS WON'T FORGET*

"One of the best worldbuilding workbooks I've ever seen. Litore is inspirational, reveling in the power of imagination and packing his journey with top-notch examples and exercises. A superb resource for beginners and pros alike." – Richard Ellis Preston, Jr., author of *Romulus Buckle and the City of the Founders*

"Stant Litore's book overflows with everything you need to know to build your own worlds from the ground up or the top down, from creatures to ecology to culture. Tons of thought-provoking exercises help create an elegant framework for speculative worldbuilding. With these techniques and your own creativity, you'll be able to create worlds your readers will never want to leave. There are other worldbuilding books out there; this is the one you want." – Travis Heermann, author of the *Ronin* trilogy and *Death Wind*

"Not only is the advice great, but there's a warmth to the chapters that makes writing inviting rather than intimidating." – Todd Mitchell, author of *The Traitor King* and *The Last Panther*

"A master class in world building: Litore has created an accessible, comprehensive approach. Covering religion, biology, technology, magic, language, justice, privilege and more, the book ignites the writer's imagination with provocative questions and exercises. Pro tip: read this with a notebook handy. You will be inspired to get down to the business of building your fictional world in ways you hadn't dreamed possible. Litore's passion for well-crafted sci-fi comes through in every chapter." – S.G. Redling, author of *Flowertown* and *Damocles*

"This is a clear, comprehensive, and beautifully written guide to worldbuilding that will not only help emerging writers to find their voices and build imaginative worlds and characters, but one that will also prove invaluable to experienced writers seeking to spark their creative impulses or deepen the worlds they create. My favorite thing about this guide was how incredibly immersive it is. When Litore says the word 'worldbuilding,' he's not kidding... Highly recommended -- I can't wait to use some of the exercises and questions Litore offers here when writing my next book." – Angela Mitchell, author of *Falada* and *Dancing Days*

"Stant Litore does an excellent job bringing structure and order to the art of world-building. His book makes the craft easy to understand and is filled with information for beginners and veterans alike." – Milton Davis, author of *Changa's Safari*

"Stant Litore is a wonderful storyteller with a knack for creating nuanced characters and equally nuanced worlds. And this book delivers on its title: it offers a great glimpse at how to write worlds your readers won't forget." – James A. Hunter, author of the *Yancy Lazarus* series and *Viridian Gate Online*

WRITE WORLDS YOUR READERS WON'T FORGET

STANT LITORE

Text copyright © 2017 Daniel Fusch.

Cover art by Roberto Calas.

Stant Litore is a pen name for Daniel Fusch.

ISBN: 9781942458302

You can reach Stant Litore at:
http://stantlitore.com
zombiebible@gmail.com
http://www.facebook.com/stant.litore
@thezombiebible

TABLE OF CONTENTS

for all you dreamers

1. How Do You Make an Unforgettable World?

LIKE A GOD, you get to invent a world. Maybe several. But how do you make these worlds that readers want to visit? How do you make them worlds that readers never want to leave? With so many fantasy and science fiction worlds out there (it's a big universe), how do you make your imagined world unforgettable? What does an unforgettable world consist of? How much detail do you plan into it, and how much of that detail do you then share with the reader?

That is what this book is intended to help you with. There are a few things you should know about this book before you begin. It is a companion to my toolkit *Write Characters Your Readers Won't Forget*, and like that book, this book is designed as a course. It is not an encyclopedia for worldbuilding but an intensive crash course. It is designed to: 1) provide you with a powerful general approach to the design of imagined worlds and 2) equip you with specific strategies for carrying out that approach and achieving rapid and exhilarating worldbuilding. There are 33 exercises in the book; I encourage you to do them, because they will help you expand the effects you are capable of achieving in your own stories. Finally, this is not a book that treats worldbuilding as a sort of academic exercise, separate from developing unforgettable characters and writing exciting, suspenseful plots. This book treats worldbuilding as a process for identifying opportunities for conflict and exerting pressures on your characters. Unforgettable characters live unforgettable stories that are made necessary and possible by the unforgettable worlds they are trying to survive and thrive in. That's the thinking behind this book.

Throughout the book, I'll present this approach to world-creation as though you are creating an entire fantasy world, alien planet, or other biosphere that is separate from our own, contemporary version of the earth. But of course there are also opportunities to create an unforgettable, imaginary world other than creating an entire new planet. You could create a magical underworld that exists on present day earth, as many urban fantasy novels do. You could create a cyberpunk future (a technological, rather than a magical, underworld). Or you could create an alternate history. These involve considerable worldbuilding, even though you aren't creating a planet. Most of this book will still be very relevant, as you will still want to ask many of the same questions when designing that underworld or alternate version of this world. You will still want to determine the physical conditions for survival in that world, populate it with remarkable creatures (though in some stories, these creatures may be machines rather than organisms), and write a memorable culture, some of whose details are different from those we know. More on that in a few pages.

In this first chapter, I'll introduce two general approaches to worldbuilding. Spoiler alert: we're going to spend the rest of the book digging into how to take the *second* approach and do it well and in ways that excite both the writer and the reader. But we'll look at "Approach A" first, because when we say "worldbuilding," Approach A is what many writers think of, and it's why many people find worldbuilding daunting or bewildering rather than utterly, rambunctiously fun.

So here it is. Approach A.

APPROACH A: FROM THE FOUNDATION UP

I want to talk first about the elephant (or the Oliphaunt) in the room, and that is J.R.R. Tolkien and the making of Middle-Earth. Creators of fantasy worlds often look to Tolkien's worldbuilding as a gold standard—usually to be either emulated or challenged. So let's take a page or two here at the start to look at Tolkien's worldbuilding process to understand how it was unique and what you can learn from it. That said, I will suggest that setting out to emulate Tolkien's process—even if you are inspired by its result— may not be very effective or realistic for many emerging speculative fiction writers. There are other ways to tackle worldbuilding, and those are what we will spend most of the book discussing and experimenting with.

Tolkien pursued his project with a total commitment that spanned decades of work. He approached worldbuilding by understanding deeply, inside and out, to a rigorous and scholarly extent, one foundational level of what makes up the cultural and social architecture of a world—its *language*. As a gifted philologist, he created (and wrote in) imaginary languages. Quite a few of them, in fact. As a young writer, he played with the differences, for example, between two elven languages that he created. Each word had an etymology, and that meant each word had a story. So he began creating stories to explain how these languages evolved, what kind of world those languages were describing. All of Middle-Earth with which we are familiar—from Frodo Baggins to Rivendell to Smaug the Dragon to the Balrogs—is derived from that impulse. Create a simulation of a living language (or more than one), a language that evolves over time, and then tell stories of how that linguistic evolution occurred.

It's an incredible experiment—one that I don't think has ever been attempted to that degree by another writer or worldbuilder. And clearly, it was effective. It is also, of course, difficult to imitate. (I mean the *process* is difficult to imitate; one can imitate a *result*, either well or badly.) It is theoretically possible for you to create an unforgettable imaginary world in the same way that J.R.R. Tolkien did if you have advanced education or deep training in one particular field relevant to worldbuilding, plus an inquisitive mind that is always asking questions about how your area of expertise informs and is informed by others. For example, if you are a gifted economist, you might begin building a world from the ground up if you start by designing a unique and detailed, though fictional, economy. If you are a biologist, you might start designing an ecosystem in meticulous detail, much as Tolkien designed languages in deep detail. This kind of deep dive is rare because it requires more than just a "research phase" to inform a novel or screenplay. It relies on committed, dedicated expertise and conversation with other experts in that area of knowledge.

That said, if you, dear colleague-writer, have a great deal of expertise and stature in some relevant field, why *not* start there? I'm not advising against it. Why not design that aspect of your fictional world first, comprehensively, A-Z, and then build the rest of the world on top of it?

APPROACH B: TWEAKING THE FLOORPLAN

However, you may not be J.R.R. Tolkien, and you may not intend the writing of your novel to be a lifelong endeavor. Most storytellers take shortcuts, and many nevertheless create unforgettable worlds in which unforgettable characters live unforgettable stories. These "shortcuts" still entail a ferocious amount of work (of the kind that is also fun), but not necessarily five to six *decades* of work. As I stressed in my earlier book *Write Characters Your Readers Won't Forget*, what grounds the reader in an exciting story is not the amount of detail you provide; it's offering the *right* details. That's what I hope this course will illustrate and clarify.

So what are these shortcuts?

Many science fiction and fantasy writers create worlds that are very much like our own, but have a handful of details that are dramatically different. That's the shortcut: Rather than lay a comprehensive foundation (linguistic or otherwise) on which to build a world, these writers insert *select but significant details* around which the rest of the world is sketched. It's like saying, "Imagine a house. You know what a house looks like. This house, however, has no roof and is open to the stars and weather; whenever it rains, tentacles reach out of the walls; and the family living in this house have organized their entire lives around the necessity of tentacle evasion."

Rather than build from the ground up, these writers take the existing world "template" that we all know and recognize and change perhaps three things—but those three things are so momentous that the rest of the world warps into a new shape around them. No roof, tentacles reaching out of the walls when it rains, a daily schedule built around getting out of the tentacles' way: three details that make this house memorable and strikingly different from other houses we have seen before. The rest of your worldbuilding is then a creative exercise in discovering and designing a world in which these three details are believable (perhaps even inevitable). I would call these three details "dramatically different details" or "overriding details."

Broadly speaking, there are three areas of worldbuilding in which a writer can insert a dramatically different detail:

1. The world's physical environment – that is, the physical conditions for survival on that world.
2. The kind of creatures that inhabit the world.
3. The cultures that inhabit and interpret that world.

In our "house" analogy, those three things are: *no roof; tentacles when it rains; tentacle-avoiding family culture*. If you are working with a planet instead of a house, then your three details may be writ larger; we'll look at examples in a minute.

Most of the time, an SF/F writer will "tweak" just one of these three. This tends to produce an unforgettable creature or an unforgettable society, but doesn't always produce an entire world that you will never forget. For example, in *The Legacy of Heorot* by Niven, Pournelle, and Barnes, a shipful of colonists settle on an earth-like planet inhabited by an array of animals that appear familiar at first glance (some fish-like things that are analogous to salmon, for example). But then Niven, Pournelle, and Barnes introduce *one* animal that is unforgettable and generates the plot for the story: the grendel, a carnivorous, amphibian creature that hyper-oxygenates its own blood for unbelievable bursts of speed and ferocity. This creature can literally burn itself to a crisp in a burst of speed, and it is both lethal and wildly difficult to kill. It provides material for a great monster-hunt story. (Niven, Pournelle, and Barnes add in a number of biological surprises: the salmon-like fish turn out to be grendel larvae, as well as the primary food source for the mature members of their species, so that once the colonists succeed in exterminating the dozen adult grendels they find, they are besieged with tens of thousands of baby grendels.)

Readers aren't likely to remember the *world* that these three co-authors created. I can't even recall the name of the colonists' planet; I would have to look it up. Nor do I recall much about the colonists' culture. I just remember the grendels. So the authors succeeded in creating an unforgettable animal/alien/monster. For the most part, they replicated our own world on the page but inserted one dramatic new biological element in order to create a thrilling science-fiction "monster" story.

By contrast, the truly unforgettable *worlds* are often the result of inserting one dramatic new element in each of the three areas of worldbuilding. So there is at least one thing that's dramatically different about the world's physical conditions; there is at least one life-form that is dramatically (not just incrementally) different; and there is one overriding difference about at least one culture that inhabits that world. There may be many minor differences, but in each area, there is one difference of such scope that it evokes wonder, beauty, or horror.

Let's look at some examples.

Dune (Frank Herbert)

Physical conditions: The planet is entirely desert. It has no precipitation. Its sands do, however, conceal a super-valuable resource (the spice).

Biology: Sandworms tunnel through the desert, creating the sand and producing both the spice and oxygen for other organisms to breathe. And these aren't just any worms: they often exceed four hundred meters in length!

Culture: The Fremen have shaped their entire lives around the necessity of conserving water. They wear stillsuits to preserve the water their body loses in sweat and urine. They do not cry, as tears would waste water. To spit at another's feet is a profound gift of water, an honor rather than an insult. They process the bodies of the dead for water (to the horror of cultures less familiar with life on Dune). And to cover the vast distances between artificial oases, they travel on the backs of the giant sandworms.

Wow, now that's a world.

We might call these three details (*desert planet; giant sandworms; culture designed to conserve water*) the organizing principles for Frank Herbert's worldbuilding. The rest of the world's design (its religions, languages, modes of transport, conflicts, etc.) proceed from these three organizing principles. Notice also that the three "details" that Herbert tweaked ... were tweaked in an extreme fashion. An entirely-desert world, sandworms larger than spaceships, and a culture that recycles its own dead for the water needed for survival ... these are extravagant changes. They invite our wonder and our curiosity. They add up to an unforgettable world, which Frank Herbert then populates with unforgettable characters and a thrilling story.

Pern (Anne McCaffrey)

Physical conditions: Every two hundred years, the planet is assailed by space-borne spores that unspool into lethal, shining clumps of "Thread." The Threads tumble down through the atmosphere to entangle and devour any organic life they touch; a single Thread can reduce an entire field to ash.

Biology: There are gigantic (Boeing-airplane-big) genetically engineered dragons who can burn Threads out of the air and can teleport from one location to another in order to counter this menace that falls from the sky.

Culture: The Pernese are highly cautious of allowing anything green to grow unchecked. Life must be sheltered under the safety of rock, and vegetable growth must be burned or uprooted, to leave fewer chances for Threads to burrow and destroy. The dragonriders maintain this law and are revered, hated, or envied by the earthbound.

Again, an unforgettable world. Notice that in both cases—Dune and Pern—there is a sequential logic to the worldbuilding. You imagine a world with demanding physical conditions, and then the wondrous animals that you can put in that world, and then cultures that must respond to those environmental conditions and to whom the marvelous animals you have created serve as either perils or resources (or both). Of course, as we'll often see in this book, you can also reverse that sequence. You could start, for example, with an animal and then imagine the world that would render that animal's existence logical or even necessary. Or you could start with a custom and then imagine the conditions for survival that would render that custom necessary or attractive to your imaginary culture.

Two things to note here before we continue.

First, when we talk about introducing readers to an imaginary civilization by means of striking and unforgettable customs, it's important that you don't mistake this for an instruction to "other" your characters and their cultures. That is, I recommend that you don't focus on making your imaginary culture "exotic"; this is a trap, one that frequently leads to a story populated by stereotypes rather than characters, and packed with tropes rather than unforgettable scenes that dramatize unique encounters. Aspects of the civilization in your novel may seem strange to the reader at first, but in most cases your ultimate goal will not be *strangeness*; your goal will likely be to bridge that strangeness for the reader and show them that the world you have created is as familiar as it is unforgettable. Great fiction doesn't *other* or *exoticize* its characters; instead, it invites the reader to experience kinship even in the midst of great difference.

Second, although in most of this book we will discuss creature design as though we are creating unforgettable animal species, the unforgettable creatures in your world may not be animal organisms. They may be sentient partner-species; in Anne McCaffrey's fiction, the intelligent dragons live in symbiosis with the Pernese. They may be plants. They may be invading alien species. They may be gods. They may be machines, like the Death Star. They may even be the restless dead. For example:

The Charter World / Ancelstierre (Garth Nix)

Physical conditions: Above the Wall, magic works. South of the Wall, it is less potent. The nearer the Wall you get, the less likely it is that your technology will work.

Spectrabiology: The dead can come back, and especially malevolent spirits can raise armies of zombies to throw at the living.

Culture: This WWI-era culture depends on necromancers (who are few) trained to step into the waters of death with their magical bells and silence the restless evils from beyond the grave.

As Garth Nix's *Sabriel* demonstrates, when given a good story to inhabit, an undead sorcerer-spirit with a hunger for humans can be just as compelling as a giant sandworm or a teleporting, telepathic dragon. The core framework, however is the same: one critical detail each is different in the physical conditions, the "biology," and the culture of this world.

Or how about this one:

The Toxic City, in *Borne* (Jeff Vandermeer)

Physical conditions: The planet after climate change is a toxic world, polluted but beautiful (those colors)! The rising seas have drowned many islands.

Creatures: Mord, a genetically-engineered, titanic flying bear, emerges periodically from the poisoned ruins to float over the city, bringing destruction.

Culture: Scavengers live in the ruins, setting traps, preying on each other, even climbing Mord's sides while he sleeps to pick useful items out of his fur: the genetically engineered organisms and tools that have clung to his fur during his rest in the subterranean ruins of the facility that had originally engineered him.

Mord is certainly unforgettable! To introduce us to this world and its eerie constraints, the book opens with a scene in which the narrator is climbing up the side of the sleeping bear, in desperate search for items she can scavenge that will make her life and her lover's more bearable and perhaps prolonged. She is anxious lest the bear awake and destroy them all. And she is armored against the toxins and poisons of a city that is only barely more habitable than the badlands outside it. The moment we open that chapter, we know we are entering a world we won't soon forget.

There are also cases in which the remarkable "creature" is also the protagonist—or one of the main characters. We see this frequently in the superhero story and in vampire fiction. So Spiderman is both "creature" and "hero." So, too, Wolverine. And Louis in *Interview with the Vampire.* In these cases, too, much of the story's drama is rooted in how the fictional culture responds to the creature, and vice versa; the difference is simply in the viewpoint perspective through which you are watching that drama play out.

A variation on this creature/hero doubling can be seen in paranormal romance and romantic SF, where the unforgettable creature is also the love interest or object of desire. While it is possible to write an SF love story with an unforgettable creature that isn't necessarily set in an unforgettable world, some examples do entail some remarkable worldbuilding. Consider the case of Gabriel in Sharon Shinn's *Archangel*, set in the distant future on the planet Samaria:

Samaria (Sharon Shinn)

Physical conditions: Above the world is a giant orbital satellite called Jovah, worshipped by the world's inhabitants as a god. This orbital satellite listens each year for the choral ceremony by which the world's peoples proclaim that they are still at peace, and will burn the world to a crisp if the ceremony does not occur.

Creatures: Genetically engineered angels, designed for flight and for musical grandeur, whose task each year is to lead the global choir that sings to the orbital satellite. Gabriel is the Archangel, the lead singer.

Culture: Marriages in this culture are arranged by interfaces with the god Jovah, presumably for genetic purposes. Additionally, the culture is very caste-stratified, with the "angels" on the mountain peaks and rigidly delineated castes below them. There's a slavery problem. And with a thermonuclear god in orbit ready to burn the world to crisp, there is a strong disincentive against revolution and against the various upheavals that are generally required in order to upset such systemic inequity.

On the bright side, musicians are held in high honor—so there's that.

From these varied examples, I hope you can see how authors of speculative fiction can select overriding details and then create from them the pressures that will be exerted on their characters and plotlines. Note that I speak of *pressures*, not *settings*. In the storyteller's kitchen, the imaginary world is the pressure cooker. Its job is to exert specific degrees of pressure and heat on the story, and to do so in the most delicious (that is, wondrous and entertaining) manner possible. All right, hold that thought. Now it's your turn to play:

Exercise 1

Pluck a few of your favorite SF/F worlds from your shelf (or bring them up on your kindle). For each of your favorites, identify the "overriding details" about the world's physical conditions, biology, and culture(s)—the details that drive that world. Next, jot down a few notes about how those details shape the kinds of characters who can inhabit that world, and the kinds of stories that can be told in that world. You are already looking at one such story with one such cast of characters. What other characters could inhabit that world? What other kinds of stories could be told? What fan fiction could this world produce?

Conversely, are there stories that would be harder to tell on this particular imaginary world? If so, why? This isn't a frivolous exercise; it's an invitation to take a closer look at how worlds shape the stories that can happen on them.

And while we're at it:

Exercise 2

Make three worlds by identifying, for each, three overriding or "dramatically different" details. I will give you the first one; you then supply the unique fact of biology and unique fact of culture that completes our basic sketch of the world:

World #1: This world is a Dyson Sphere: a massive, artificial sphere completely enclosing a sun. The inhabited "world" is on the sphere's interior hull, facing the sun.

World #2: There is no landmass. The world is completely covered in water.

World #3: The planet has extremely high oxygen content in the atmosphere, so that wildfires are devastating and the evolution of organisms of prodigious and extraordinary size is both possible and likely.

For each of these three, imagine at least one extravagant and surprising creature, and imagine at least one unique detail about what kind of culture has developed either to survive or thrive amidst the physical conditions and the creatures on that world.

Now, look at the three imaginary worlds you have created. What characters could you imagine living in (or resisting) those imaginary cultures? What kinds of stories could you tell in each of those worlds? Which story could you tell in each world that would be most exciting?

This may sound like a very basic framework, but as you have seen in the examples above, from *Dune* to *Borne*, identifying these three details can empower some remarkably nuanced work.

Conditions for survival/creature design/culture: We're going to use this as the organizing framework for this course. In the next several chapters, we will walk through each of these three areas in much more detail, looking at examples of what playful creativity and a little knowledge in each of these areas can produce. Practical exercises throughout these chapters will invite you to seize these opportunities and see what happens. Then, in Chapter 5, we'll discuss strategies for sharing your imagined world effectively with your readers.

Hold on tight to your dragon, sandworm, or bandolier of necromantic bells, because there be wonders—and monsters—ahead. Turn the page, and let's go take a look.

2. CONDITIONS FOR SURVIVAL

ONE GOOD WAY TO BEGIN is to identify an ecological or planetological constraint. Our survival is dictated by our access to those resources critical to life (oxygen, food, water) and by the sufficient absence of conditions inimical to life (extreme heat, extreme cold, radiation, toxins in the air or water, etc.). So one way to exert pressure on the characters who will inhabit your world (and set the conditions for thrilling stories) is to dial down the access to critical resources or dial up the presence of lethal elements.

This isn't the *only* way to begin, however. You could also start by dialing the access to resources way, way *up*—create a world where there is always sunlight, for example. A jungle world. Or a world where it rains four hundred and seventy-two days out of a five-hundred-day year. Then play with the psychological and cultural effects of living in such a world. In Asimov's "Nightfall," on the one day in a thousand years when all the suns set, people panic and burn cities to the ground in their desperation to produce light. In Bradbury's "The Long Rains," explorers from earth who visit a planet of unending precipitation gradually go insane in their need for the rain to stop pelting them.

Here is a portrait of a world I painted in "Ansible 15717," a world both more biodiverse and beautiful than our own and more deadly:

> There are no discernible seasons here, which is strange to me. Botany is all about seasons. But here the plants just *grow*, sweating moisture in the dawn heat. I have never seen such plants on earth or any of its colonies, not even in the hydroponics bays on the moon that provide most of the food for our teeming billions. How can I possibly describe it…think of the rain forests your grandmothers told you about, the forests our planet once had but that our ancestors butchered, the ones you think are at least half mythical, where rose trees grew a hundred fifty feet high, and a thousand species of butterflies might flourish in the canopy of a single tree, waking Allah from his dreaming with their riot of hues. Think of the old vidcasts you saw in school, slow-motion capture of frogs leaping from a pool, their skin like wet paint. Back when there were frogs. Think of that. Hold those images, images of an alien world that somehow bore the same name as our own, hold those in your mind.
>
> Then imagine a forest ten times that intense, one that could make a botanist who has harbored a secret atheism all her life suddenly kneel, head to the ground, and pray. Think of an entire ecosystem of miniature forests growing *inside* the hollow bole of a tree the size of a spaceport. Then imagine that the tree of such prodigious vitality is not even a *tree*, but only a kind of flowering weed with an exterior harder than bark, harder than granite. Imagine a single nocturnal blossom that would fill the Al-Masjid al-Haram from one wall to the other, that each night spews into the air millions of airborne spores that burn with light like violet sparks; all it would take is the feather-soft touch of

just one against the back of your hand, and you would be dead before you could even gasp.

This is a world of beauty and strange poisons. An entire species of botanists could not fully catalogue it.

Even on our own earthly world, conditions for survival vary drastically from one climate to another. So what are the conditions for survival on your world? If it is a more abundant world than ours, do you play that up in order to evoke wonder? How do you create opportunities for tension in that world?

So one thing to think about is the availability of life-critical resources and the presence of conditions inimical to life. Now try this:

Exercise 3

Choose a life-critical resource and dial it as far up as you can imagine. What creatures and what people might populate such a world?

Then take the same resource and dial its availability as far *down* as you can imagine without prohibiting life entirely. Who will exist on this world of extreme scarcity, and how?

Next, let's consider the geography and structure of your world.

EITHER SIDE OF THE RIVER

A colleague of mine, Lucy, once told me about a college course she took, now many decades ago. The professor assigned the students the task of writing an essay on the thesis that in the age of modern warfare, the minute facts of geography were no longer relevant. (Clearly, this professor had never served in the military, or spoken with many veterans.)

Lucy, being a rebel, submitted for her essay a short story in which a journalist is interviewing refugees from a devastating invasion. There is a battle still raging in the background. At one point, the journalist thrusts a mic in a medic's face, and the medic, exasperated at the interruption of his critical, life-saving work, turns on the reporter and shouts: "All right! You want to know why these people are fighting? Because *this* tribe has lived for thousands of years on *this* side of the river, and *that* tribe has lived for thousands of years on *that* side of the river. That's why!"

Lucy received an A+ on her short story.

Geography isn't just something to learn by rote, or a set of background details for your worldbuilding. Geography can shape the conditions for survival. It can define or limit possibilities for conflict. It can provide opportunities for suspense—quite simply, for things to go dramatically wrong in entertaining ways. And, as Lucy shared with me, geography doesn't just determine the shape of warfare and conflict; it shapes history.

Consider Earth's history. In the deep Amazon rain forest, we still have "uncontacted" peoples. Films and stories have been written about the conflict and danger of the encroachment of modern civilization on those rain forests, focused on perils from disease to deforestation.

On the opposite side of the geographical spectrum, consider ancient Egypt, a civilization that was in contact with nearly *everybody* and had access to an invaluable natural resource: the fertile Nile floodplain that provided a regular excess of storable food. Egypt is the Greek name for that country; the Egyptians named their own country *Kemet*, the "dark earth," meaning the very fertile soil. That's a mark of the extent to which the seasonal flooding of the Nile River shaped their lives and their experience of the world.

But Kemet grew up from villages to cities on either side of the river. A little way to the west or east of the river, you ran into desert and empty, untillable land. So you had a nation that consisted of towns on two sides of a river with all this empty land on either side and no other natural defenses. And this nation possessed an invaluable resource. This meant that Egypt was fabulously wealthy and people were able to live in great comfort there—but also that Egypt was constantly being invaded: by the Hittites, the Sea Peoples, the Ethiopians, later by the Greeks and the Persians and the Romans and the Arabs and the Turks. So to protect its people, Egypt became the first country in human history to keep a standing army.

Think about how geography will shape the conditions for survival, for conflict, for economy in *your* imagined world.

Are there mountains? If so, do your characters live in the dry rain shadow, or on the slopes where rain is frequently dumped out of the sky?

What resources are available to your people? What resources do they need? What can they trade to get what they need? If someone tries to take it from them, what will they do? If resources are scarce, how is it decided who gets them? How does the economy work in your world?

Or consider a more fantastical geography. In Joseph Brassey's *Skyfarer*, the "infinite sky" is sparsely populated by floating islands and continents. The vast distances between these levitating landmasses is crossable only by use of portals created by skilled mages. This in turn necessitates academies and universities for the training of such mages. This in turn provides occasion for different classes and subcultures in that world. There are "skyfarers"—who are born and live and study in the infinite sky, leaping across immeasurable distances—and there are the groundborn.

C.J. Cherryh digs into similar dynamics in great detail (and to great effect) in her *Chanur* and *Alliance/Union* novels, in which much of the story and the conflict is driven by the differences between "stationer" cultures and "ship" cultures.

The structure and the geography of your imagined world shape culture, and they shape character. Try these exercises:

Exercise 4

This imagined world is an endless city. Your character has never seen greenery. Now, write the three paragraphs immediately following a scene in which your character tumbles through a portal unexpectedly into the heart of an old-growth forest on another world. What is your character's reaction? Are they struck by overwhelming beauty and color, alien to their gray, urban world? Are they terrified? What details might you add to these paragraphs to strengthen their reaction? Is there a pleasing scent to the moss in the forest? Is it the middle of the night—do they have to scramble with the batteries of their flashlight? Is the forest silent, especially for a character who is used to the hum of electricity, the background noise of their existence that has now been suddenly and entirely removed? How do they even begin to understand what they are seeing? How do they feel about it? Write those three paragraphs.

Exercise 5

Your character has lived all her life inside a space station with walls and ceiling close around her. Suddenly, she wakes on a planet with an endless sky above her. Write the three paragraphs following her waking. How does she feel? How does she react? Does she squeeze her eyes shut and pray? Does she cling to the grass, terrified she will fall into the sky? Or is her response something other than shock and fear? How has her space-station culture prepared her or failed to prepare her with ways to understand this experience? Write those three paragraphs.

As you can see here, contrasting two different worlds with two different environments can be an effective way to understand either of those worlds better, and to understand how that world shapes the lives that inhabit it.

You can also explore how geography might affect natural (or supernatural) perils in your world. In Garth Nix's *Sabriel*, a lot of suspense is created by the necessity of our protagonist's race to cross running water—because the dead can't follow her across a river. In my own *Zombie Bible*, the mindless dead follow the path of least resistance as they stumble across the landscape. Like water, the herds of dead flow downhill. This is bad news if there is a plague uphill from you. It means that tribes in the hill country remain loosely nomadic, ready to pack up their tents at a moment's notice, whereas cities in the plain build high walls that they can hide their people behind. And in the city of Rome on its seven hills, the dead flow downhill toward the river—which means that the ghettos of the poor bear the worst brunt of the infestation, while the rich hide within their stately villas…until people begin fleeing *up*hill, drawing hungry dead after them.

The natural world has its perils, too. If there are carnivorous dragons in your world, what determines their hunting grounds or their migratory patterns? If there is dry grassland or dry forest and a risk of wildfire, in what direction do the prevailing winds move? Where will the fire *go*, and toward whom, in your world?

So think about *distance*, *direction*, and *barriers* (like a river to block the dead). Most of all, remember how geography influences the living habits of peoples and the perils they face. Some imaginary cultures build cities with high walls, some live in tents, some fly on ships between floating continents—but none of it is arbitrary. Imaginative and fun, yes, but also purposeful. Discover the constraints under which your world operates and the shape and structure of your world that determines how those constraints can be addressed—and you have opportunities for conflict and story.

TAKING ONE SCENE
AND REVERSE-ENGINEERING A WORLD

For the purpose of offering tips and instruction, in this book I'm treating worldbuilding almost as though it is an exercise you complete *before* writing the story. But of course it may not be—and it may not need to be, and it may not be wise for it to be. Depending on your own process, a lot of what we're talking about can be reverse-engineered. Understanding how you can engineer an imaginary world in detail empowers us to do that, to engage in worldbuilding at any point in our storytelling (and that is why this book, I hope, will be useful).

Maybe the first thing you imagine is a scene. Maybe you imagine a tribe of elves fleeing a dragon. And now you want to make that story more exciting, more detailed, and more deeply imagined by the reader. You want to write the most exciting elves-fleeing-a-dragon scene that you possibly can. So you can start building out the world around that scene by asking yourself world-engineering questions, focusing on identifying what aspects of this world will exert pressures on either the elves' flight or the dragon's pursuit. For example, you could explore:

- What *obstacles* are in the way of the fleeing elves?
- What *barriers* might they find or create, to protect themselves from this dragon? (Do they need to get underground? Do they need to get under cover of trees? Or will the dragon just burn them out?)
- What *tools* can they harness in the natural landscape? (Are there particular organisms that frighten dragons, as tribbles do Klingons, that your elves can find? Are there poisons they can access, to dip their arrows in, but only in a certain part of the landscape, or only at a certain time?

Do those poisonous flowers only bloom and become visible by the light of a full moon?)

- Are there ways that the *physics* of this world may come into play? (Is there lower gravity than our world? Can elves glide for short distances? Etc.)

Exercise 6

Time for action scenes! Briefly sketch, write, or draw what a battle between a tribe of elves and a dragon might look like on each of the following worlds:

a) A low-gravity world on which an elf can leap a hundred feet.

b) An earth-gravity thunder-world of eternal cloud cover and eternal rain.

c) A world completely covered in forest, with trees a thousand feet tall, where dragon and elves live their entire lives beneath a thick forest canopy.

d) A volcanic world where elves and dragon battle on islands of rock surrounded by rivers and lakes of lava, where the air is full of fumes and near-lethal heat.

In each of these four cases, how do the physical conditions of the imagined world affect the battle, the maneuvers possible, the threat and mobility of the dragon, lines of sight for archers, weapons that might be either crafted uniquely for this environment or improvised from surrounding objects in the moment, and what the elves wear *to* battle? Be creative—and most of all, have fun.

Action scenes are exciting. Why *not* start by writing an imaginative action scene and then imagine the world that would render that action possible and necessary—or a world whose conditions would make that action scene more complicated?

CLIMATE CHANGE AND CATASTROPHE

All right, before we move on to talk about creature design, let's discuss one more thing related to the physical conditions of survival in your world. How *stable* is your world? Is your world warming rapidly—or cooling rapidly, like Westeros in *A Song of Ice and Fire*? Is this a seasonal (but dramatic) change that the cultures and species in your world have adapted to, or is it a sudden and apocalyptic change? What happens to your world if a meteor hits? If a volcano erupts? If the sea levels rise and some island nations cease to exist? Do the species on those islands take to the seas by flotilla? What happens when they reach someone else's shore? What if your world's rotation is gradually slowing, like earth's in the prehistory of William Hope Hodgson's *The Night Land*—in which humanity populates vast, mobile cities that follow the sun slowly around the world?

Creating a world that is in a moment of change can provide not only physical dangers but also social and cultural ones. How do your imaginary civilizations cope with the changes coming to their world? How do they adapt? Do some deny it? What happens to those whose homes either cease to exist or are irrevocably changed? You are doubtless familiar with *nostalgia*, the pain of yearning for a home you have left; philosopher Glenn

Albrecht coined the term *solastalgia* to describe the pain of yearning for a home that has left you. That is, you are still there, still in your home, but it has been wrecked and you have been powerless to prevent the wrecking. Albrecht used the term to describe the experiences of people living in environments that were healthy, beautiful, and supportive of life within living memory but have since been devastated ecologically.

One way to think about fiction in general and worldbuilding in particular is that stories are about the process of adapting and the decisions made in order to adapt. A character resolves a conflict by changing something in themselves, making new decisions or courses of action available. You can think about worldbuilding as an activity that simultaneously defines the barriers to adaptation and the circumstances that permit your characters (and the civilizations in which they live) to adapt. You can also think about building worlds that are changing, so that the physical world is part of what the character has to adapt *to*. And you can then design a culture that has within it forces (and characters exemplifying those forces) that either encourage or resist that adaptation.

Did you see the film *Moana?* In the movie, all vegetation on the island is withering. It is happening very slowly. So there is a character who wants to act, adapt, and seek a solution (the heroine, Moana); a character who denies the crisis and wishes for the people to stay put and live as they have always done (Moana's father); and there are characters who support the heroine in her desire to adapt and venture forth. They support her either enthusiastically (her grandmother) or quietly (her mother).

29

Exercise 7

Imagine a world that is dying. Perhaps this "world" is a generational starship that has been traveling for a thousand years. It has finally reached its destination world, the world that the people of that starship were to colonize. But those people have lived on board for a thousand years. The starship doesn't have power to remain a habitat for long after the arrival. Pick a character who will lead the charge to evacuate the starship and settle the world below. Name the character. Pick a profession for them.

Now brainstorm two other characters, one who will support and one who will resist. The one resisting change will do so from a motive of loving the world they have; they don't want to leave. Motivated by this, what might they do in the story?

Pick the motive of the person supporting the protagonist; it has to be a motive different from the protagonist's. Maybe it is love for the protagonist. Maybe it is a yearning for adventure.

What kind of story might you tell, with these characters?

PLANETOLOGY, BIOLOGY, AND CULTURE ARE ALL CONNECTED

All the elements of worldbuilding—the physical conditions of your world, the creatures in it, and the cultures in it—interlock and affect each other. They are interdependent; each determines the others.

For example, the physical conditions for survival on a world and the creatures that populate that world can create the necessity for your characters to carve out specific kinds of homes. In Frank Herbert's *Dune*, the Fremen create vast cave networks with water-seals; they develop a kind of home that enables them to shelter from the desert and to come to terms with its most hostile conditions. In the urban fantasy of Jim Butcher, the onslaught of demons, vampires, and other things that go bump in the night necessitate that the wizard protagonist have a basement home that provides a bolthole with magical wards to protect it and prevent intrusion. In Robin McKinley's *Spindle's End*, the unforgettable fact about the world she creates is that the environment is so permeated with magic that the inhabitants need to constantly scrub magic off of everything, to prevent everyday activities from yielding unpredictable and chaotic results. Let too much magic encrust itself on the inside of a frying pan, and live chickens will burst from the pan instead of scrambled eggs. Or something more sinister might occur. In all these cases, the physical conditions of the world shape the idea of "home" and the management of daily life, as well as the threats the characters will encounter over the course of a novel.

Your world's unique ecology will shape the fictional *culture* deeply too. If, for example, your elves are trying to evade a nocturnal dragon while searching a swamp desperately for the poison-flowers that bloom by the full moon and that contain the only neurotoxin that can stop a full-grown dragon ... if that is the world in which your characters operate, then how has that world shaped the elves' culture? Is there an old grandmother or matriarch who is the keeper of the knowledge of the swamp-herbs? Was she injured in the dragon's first attack? Perhaps she is half-scorched and dying. Perhaps her grand-daughter must now remember everything she can from the matriarch's lessons and try, at great risk, to extract the necessary poison. Perhaps a young warrior of the tribe whose bow will be needed to fire the poisoned arrow into the dragon's eye has, in the past, scorned the grandmother and her knowledge. After all, dragons so rarely attack. Maybe it has been generations. Maybe the young archer believed the grandmother over-cautious about where the tribe should, and should not, hunt. Maybe it was the archer who alerted the dragon to the elves' presence during a hunt. Maybe it was the granddaughter, following the archer through the woods intending to court her. Maybe one of them feels guilt over the coming of the dragon and the dying of the matriarch, and must face that guilt and their own past mistakes if they are to save the people. Maybe the archer's guilt keeps her hand unsteady at the bow—what will allow her to make the true shot? Love for the young woman who gathered the poison-blossoms? A defiant affirmation of her own self-worth? The need to protect her family?

Do you see?

This is the joy of worldbuilding, whether you begin with it or whether you engage in this activity at various moments throughout the process of writing your novel. In this example, we started with a scene about elves fleeing a dragon, then began imagining the world that would exert pressures on that story of flight and pursuit, then began imagining how those pressures would shape the elves' culture. In doing this, we discovered new characters that we didn't have before—the archer, the matriarch, the granddaughter. Our story is richer and more exciting for it.

And in Chapter 3 (Creature Design) we'll look at the questions we can ask that would help us write a more exciting dragon (how do dragons actually *work* in this world?), and in Chapter 4 (Imaginary Civilizations) we'll look at the questions we can ask that would help us make a more exciting elven culture.

THE KEY POINT

I hope what I am conveying by showing you the kinds of questions you can ask in defining your world—and how these lead to additional questions—is that 1) worldbuilding is a process not only of engineering but of discovery, and that losing yourself in that joy of discovery is part of what takes you from a story set in a dull world to a story electrified by an exciting world. And 2) **worldbuilding is not an activity that is separate from plot design or character development. The conditions you write into the world create *opportunities* for plot and exert *pressures* on your characters.**

When you think about worldbuilding in this way, creating a climate can be exciting as creating a car chase. In fact, if you talk with talented screenwriters who write car chases or to writers who teach action sequences—like M. H. Boroson, author of *The Girl with the Ghost Eyes*—you will find that they create those car chases by designing little worlds. As Boroson explains, writing an unforgettable action scene is an act of worldbuilding; the writer defines the obstacles and barriers that will impose constraints on the action, the deconstructibles in the scene (that is, what parts of the environment can be smashed into or shattered during the scene for dramatic effect), and the availability of improvised tools or weapons that will make the action sequence more exciting. They build a microcosmic world in which the action can take place, and this world exerts specific pressures on the characters and provides specific opportunities that are unique to that action sequence—in other words, unique to that world.

Designing a planet is an analogous process—just bigger. Just as when you plan an action scene, you have physical barriers (the physical conditions for survival in your world), deconstructibles or items or people that can be smashed into (these are your unforgettable creatures), and improvised tools (details of your culture and society that come into play in surprising ways).

That's why Exercise 6 above can be useful to you. Writing a battle scene between elves and dragons and thinking through how the physical environment imposes constraints and opens opportunities for the characters can stretch the writerly muscles that you need for all worldbuilding, whether you are working with a single scene, a novel, or an entire series.

3. CREATURE DESIGN

IN THE EXAMPLE of the elves fleeing the dragon in the previous chapter, we discussed geographical and planetological considerations that can add urgency to the story by imposing constraints on the action. But we might also have talked about *biological* constraints that might come into play. For example, in your thrilling story of elves being pursued by a hungry dragon in your imagined world, are dragons diurnal or nocturnal? Do the elves just have to make it alive to nightfall or dawn? Do they have to get into hiding before sunset? You can create urgency if you know this.

Similarly, are the dragons warm-blooded or cold-blooded? If they are cold-blooded and require warm weather to be active, do the elves need to get up into the mountaintops, into the snow? If so, how will they keep warm and keep fed while they are up there?

Or are dragons warm-blooded and well adapted to sustained activity in cold weather? Are they thickly furred? Is there blubber under their hides? Are these *winter* dragons? Are the elves fleeing down from the mountain slopes toward the desert?

Let's talk about creature design.

EVOLUTIONARY TRADE-OFFS

Biology is about trade-offs; everything in biology has a cost, and so biology's most extravagant feats entail the most extravagant costs. The gazelle runs very fast in order to evade predators, but its long legs are brittle. On the other end of that spectrum, *le chien de montagne*, the Pyrenees mountain dog bred to protect flocks of sheep, has mass and muscle to break the bones of wolves, but male Pyrenees suffer severe hip problems late in life. Another example: The higher the metabolism, the more a creature must eat; if an animal expends vast quantities of energy, it needs to consume replacement energy. Thus the common shrew has to consume four times its own mass in a single day. The super-quick or super-ferocious may suffer other costs, as well. In *The Legacy of Heorot*, Niven, Pournelle, and Barnes imagine a carnivore capable of extreme bursts of speed, but this carnivore has to stay near water or snow in order to cool rapidly after that burst. Otherwise, the grendel will cook itself. So, in designing creatures, think of the tradeoffs.

Creatures evolve in response to environmental conditions. When our planetary atmosphere had a greater oxygen content, we had larger animals—rhinos like moving mountains, and of course dinosaurs. Not to mention, at one time, insects longer than I am tall. Those animals could not live in our atmosphere today—not enough oxygen. Creatures also evolve in response to other organisms. Fish in a pool without any predators will develop, over generations, brighter colors in order to attract mates. Fish in a pool *with* predators will be duller in color, in order to avoid being seen and eaten; they have to find the right balance between looking sexy (to other fish) and looking edible. So how do the environmental conditions on your world shape the creatures in it? (If you would like to explore evolutionary tradeoffs in more detail, a wonderful resource is the chapter "Arms races and 'evolutionary theodicy'" in Richard Dawkins' *The Greatest Show on Earth*.)

Exercise 8

Your assignment here is to create an animal that has an extravagant ability, a superhero-type ability. Maybe it can turn itself invisible, or burn a ton of energy in order to cast itself five minutes into the future in self-defense, when it is attacked. Or maybe it can run as fast as the Flash. Or maybe it can control minds. How many can it control? For how long?

Once you've decided on this animal's "superpower," come up with the cost. What is the cost of expending that energy? What parts of the animal's body are involved? What evolutionary sacrifices have been made, what vulnerabilities introduced, to make this superpower possible? These will be vulnerabilities your characters can exploit.

BIOLOGICAL IMPERATIVES

Instinct is an incredibly powerful thing. In *Dune*, the Bene Gesserit suggest that what separates the human from the animal is the human being's ability to *override* instinct, to do the smart thing even when our body is clamoring for us to do something else.

I will leave that distinction for the philosophers to ponder. But it's useful to think about it here, because it illustrates that instinct usually overrides the organism, not the other way around. What biological imperatives drive your species? And how might this animal's instincts be incredibly dangerous not only to the characters in your story but also to the animal itself? (Remember the myth of the lemmings traveling in a straight line without stopping even if there is a cliff's edge along the way.)

A great example of this appears in *A Mote in God's Eye* by Larry Niven and Jerry Pournelle. In this novel, the first extraterrestrial species contacted by humanity is one for whom the biological imperative to copulate and produce offspring is truly overwhelming. Members of that species literally die if they do not have sex. This is a leftover from their evolutionary development that, as a sentient and spacefaring species, they have not been able to abrogate. Niven and Pournelle play out the possible consequences of this biological imperative: massive overpopulation followed by inevitable crash of their civilization, leading to endless cycles of repopulation and crash, repopulation and crash, across millions of years of history.

What biological imperatives drive your imagined species? Is there a thing this species *must* do, whatever the cost, no matter what is in its way?

What about migration?

Exercise 9

Create a species that is sentient and migrates. That is, its members are self-aware, and in order to survive and obey the biological imperatives of their own bodies, they embark on years-long migrations. Answer these questions:

- How do they travel?
- What is the destination like?
- Being sentient, how do they feel about their destination?
- What happens when they arrive? Do they give birth? Do they go there to die? Is this destination the only place where their species ever mates?
- Imagine a human character, perhaps the heroine of your story. She makes a pledge to one of these other creatures, that she will accompany them on this migration. She is the only human ever to do so. What does this mean to her? What does this mean to the other humans? How do they react? How do the migratory creatures react?
- What makes this migratory journey difficult for a human being to undertake with her friend?
- What does she see on that migratory journey?
- How does it change her?

Doesn't that sound like there might be a great story ready to be born in that world! Among that species? Go find that story.

Or, after doing this exercise and learning how that world and that creature design opens up possibilities for storytelling, go and do likewise with your own imagined world.

LIFE CYCLES

We just talked about migration. What about other kinds of life cycles? What stages does your fictional organism pass through between its origin and its death? Does it progress from larva to pupa or chrysalis to mature adult? If so, does the adult look as different from the larva as a butterfly does from a caterpillar?

Exercise 10

Imagine a species that goes through a transformation as complete as caterpillar-to-butterfly. What does that transformation entail? How does the creature approach it? In what ways is the organism vulnerable during the transformation? List all the bad things that could happen to the creature while it is mid-transformation.

Then think of the characters that inhabit this imaginary world:

- If your character's task is to prevent the creature from transforming, what will your character need to do, and how difficult will it be?
- If your character's task is to protect the creature while it transforms, what will your character need to do, and how difficult will it be?
- How does this change if your character sees the creature as a god?
- How does this change if your character sees the creature as a child?

Exercise 11

Imagine a second species that goes through a transformation as complete as caterpillar-to-butterfly. This time, imagine that your creature is capable of intelligent thought and emotion. How does it handle this total transformation, this death and resurrection-as-a-new-thing? Does your character yearn for the metamorphosis, or do they desperately wish *not* to transform?

Let's suppose this organism has its own culture. Write a poem or a prayer of five or six lines that is what that creature will recite either when it goes into the chrysalis or after it comes out.

Here are a few examples of such biological (or xenobiological) life cycles to consider from science fiction and fantasy.

In *Alien*, Lieutenant Ripley encounters xenomorphs that have a complex life cycle. One form of the creature hatches from an egg and then locates a living host in which to implant the larva for the next stage in the life cycle. That larva then hatches…erupting from the human host in extremely bloody fashion. The creature then grows rapidly, shedding skins until it reaches its mature state. Much of the drama in the plot derives from some characters attempting to aid the creature in its seizure of organic hosts, while others seek to stop and destroy the creature.

In Madeleine L'Engle's *A Wind in the Door*, Meg Murray encounters the farandolae, microscopic creatures that live inside of human cells. In the story, these organisms are sentient. Their larvae are mobile and swim or scamper about. The adult form is rooted to the walls of the cell, and resembles kelp, the vast seaweed forests we find in our oceans. Much of the drama in the plot derives from the larval creatures' reluctance to lose their mobility (although, if they do not "Deepen," their species will cease to exist inside that one human cell), and the attempts of the rooted farandolae to persuade their young of the joys of adulthood for their species.

Exercise 12

Now create a species of gods. This is going to be fun! In their adult form, in this imaginary world, these gods will feed on the worship of millions and will grant those millions benefits in return for the faith they are fed.

I want you to create the theobiology for these gods. They are born and at some point they *may* die. What is their lifecycle? What is their larval state? How are they cared for during that state? Are *human beings* their larval state? Is their larval state a kind of plant? Or a fungus—like a giant mushroom? What are these larvae, and what do they do? How do they interact with their environment, and what problems might this present for some human characters in this imagined world?

Finally, what is their apotheosis—that is, their transformation from larva into full godhood—like?

Here are some more questions to ponder about your imaginary species: How does this species care for its young? On earth, animals that birth *many* young tend to focus their energies on concealing the eggs and focus less energy on the care and nurture of the offspring. It's a numbers game. Some of those baby spiders will float or crawl successfully to the site of their first web. Some of those baby turtles will make it down to the sea. Conversely, animals (including humans) that produce few young tend to invest considerable energy in the nurture and protection of each of those young, ensuring that as many as possible reach maturity safely (and hopefully well-prepared for life as mature members of their species).

How is birth achieved? Sequoia redwoods, many of them thousands of years old, clone themselves; thousands of clone cells burst into green saplings when the old tree dies. If your creatures gestate their young, as mammals do, does that mean temporary vulnerability on the part of the one doing the gestating? How does the species compensate for this vulnerability? For example, marsupials compensate by shortening the time of gestation; they birth their young early and then carry them in pouches while they finish developing, allowing the females to shorten the gestational period and return to optimal mobility and grazing as quickly as possible. Seahorses take a different approach, switching duties from one sex to the other midway through, splitting the difference, so that the male carries the offspring during the final stages of the gestational cycle.

What are the obstacles to birth? Is nesting needed? Do your aquatic but air-breathing creatures need to lift their offspring to the surface, as whales do? What dangers does this present, if so? Or—horribly—is there a creature that lays its eggs within sentient hosts, as some wasps do, or like those xenomorphs in *Alien*?

So many delightful (or horrid; your mileage may vary) questions! It is not a bad idea to keep a biology textbook around and peruse it frequently, to remind yourself of some of these questions. Or to befriend a biologist. Or to look up the *oddest* terrestrial creatures of which you are aware and then pay close attention to how their biology works and why they exist the way that they do. In other words, practice stretching your imagination. Here on our own earth, the diversity in how organisms exist and survive and thrive is incredible. If you're going to bring another world into the mix, be as creative as you can!

And do the unexpected. Here is my nod toward the amphibian lifecycle of dragons, in my book *Dante's Heart*:

> Sometimes, he would run out even beyond the acre of wood to where the land dipped and there were deep ponds. When his mother yet lived, she used to enjoy going down there to watch the marsh birds, but she never went in the rain. That was Dante's time. He would find a decaying log and lie down on it and watch that dark water in which swam the tadpoles of dragons, sleek and black and large enough to fill his cupped hands if he wanted to lift one wriggling from the water. In the summer when their legs began to grow, his father had to come down to the ponds to kill them or there would be dragons everywhere. But one or two always made it. These would live shy and massive in the wood, and the next spring the ponds would be full of their tadpoles again, beautiful and round with long tails. When it rained, they would rise to the surface like dark koi mistaking the splash of raindrops for the arrival of insects and thinking of food. Dante remembered their round faces and glassy eyes just below the surface,

things from another time, imbued with the grace of silent dancers.

Bet you haven't thought of dragons having tadpoles before. What surprises can *you* astonish your readers (and your characters) with?

THE EXCITEMENT OF ECOLOGY

Now the *really* fun stuff.

Organisms don't just inhabit their environments; they *change* them. Beavers transform arid territory into lush lake lands. Locusts strip fields bare. Redwoods soak in water and survive fires and grow tall above the ashes of lesser trees, until they create a forest that is *only* redwoods. And giant sandworms on Dune grind the soil into sand and replenish the planet's air from the furnaces of their interior oxygen factories. And then there are humans—don't even get me started.

Near the beginning of this chapter, I asked, "How do the environmental conditions on your world shape the creatures in it?" Now I want to ask, "How do the creatures on your world shape its environmental conditions?"

How do *your* imagined creatures, or monsters, or gods, alter their environments? This completely works for gods, too. In a fantasy world, do the gods occasionally strike mountains into plains or raise plains into mountains? Do they bring fertility or remove it and bring famine, like Ostara in the televised adaption of *American Gods*? Do they occasionally get royally pissed off and smack the ocean with their fist and create tidal waves? There is a fantasy world I am continually dabbling at and will one day publish stories in, in which the presence of the gods distorts time, so that a man carries freshly killed caribou back from the hunt to feed his people only to find them years dead, or a woman wakes from a night with her lover to find that no one remembers him having been born.

How might the removal of a creature shape the world? Worlds are complex ecological systems, and each item in that system matters. And don't neglect the non-animal. As noted above, redwoods have a dramatic impact on their world, and maybe your elves choose them as their sacred trees not only because they are pretty but because the redwood are truly the gods of the forest, under whose shadow other trees burn and wither and perish. Maybe you have carnivorous plants. Maybe your world—like our prehistoric earth, long ago—is covered in forests not of trees but of fungal pillars. Maybe a particular airborne fungus can land in animals' fur, corrupting the innocent animals of your world and turning them into mindless destructive machines (for the sole purpose of spreading fungal spores everywhere), and your world's culture has established methods, weapons, and entire warrior sisterhoods to deal with that recurring peril. Perhaps their very houses and homes have been designed to deal adaptively with this unique peril.

Exercise 13

Write one scene each that explores the following scenarios:

1. When it rains, tentacle-beasts slouch out of the swamps. Let's suppose these tentacular swamp-dwellers have the ability to pry their way into any surface that is moist, peeling open a tiny crack and squeezing themselves through like octopi—even if the opening they have found is only a centimeter thick. And on this fictional planet, it rains constantly. To defend themselves, your characters have had to construct specific kinds of homes. Imagine what homes have been developed to adapt to this threat, and write a scene in which the characters flee to safety in those homes.

2. This time, let's start with a house and reverse-engineer a creature-threat and an ecology. In this world, your characters design homes that have zero reflective surfaces. No mirrors, no shiny metal or glass, nothing that can give back a reflection. Think, also, about how they gather water for their houses without risking any contact with a reflection. What are they sheltering from? And if this creatures requires reflections, think about the world in which it exists—is it a world where reflective surfaces are extremely common? A world of vast still lakes, or groves of multi-faceted tree-like structures made of glass? Write a scene that reveals the organism to which your characters have adapted.

NOW, LET'S DESIGN THAT DRAGON

All right. Back to our elves fleeing the dragon. Let's suppose we bring in the amphibian dragon that we met earlier in this chapter. Or one rather like it. Maybe this is specifically a *swamp* dragon, a worm of the fens, submerged like a crocodile in the muck and the mire but much faster and larger and more brutal than any crocodile. And maybe this dragon shares no common biology with crocodile or dinosaur; maybe *this* dragon on *this* world is an amphibian. A hundred-foot-long super-newt grown from a tadpole the size of your fist. A marsh-salamander hungry for elves, spending much of its life span in the water but with great fins at its side that render it, on this low-gravity world, capable of brief and awe-inspiring flights. Maybe the existence of this amphibian dragon is even why there *are* such prodigious marshes on this world; maybe these dragons, beaver-like, have built dams and lodges from weeds and muck and fallen trees, to trap the water and terraform sections of the landscape to be more habitable for their species.

Remember when we discussed climate change in Chapter 2? One way to insert a catastrophe into your world is to introduce an invasive species. Then our characters have to respond and adapt and survive. If our amphibian dragons are changing their world into a swamp, the next question is: How will our dry-forest elves adapt? How will their culture understand what's happening? What cherished beliefs will be challenged by the swamping of the land? What stories become possible in that time of change?

That's the subject of our next chapter.

4. IMAGINARY CIVILIZATIONS

Each section in this chapter provides a strategy for designing or discovering your imagined civilization. You don't need to pursue them all, but each strategy offers a different window you can peer through to see more of your imagined world—a different way to understand your alien civilization and the opportunities for storytelling that the uniqueness of that fictional culture makes possible.

LET'S GO BACK TO our tale of elves fleeing the dragon. At this point, maybe we have imagined an exciting physical world for them to flee through and interact with, a world of vast swamps and poison-flowers. And we have imagined a unique and breathtaking kind of dragon, a dragon no one has ever seen before, a dragon adapted for swamps and a *creator* of swamps.

Now we have the world. We have the dragon. We just need the elves. We need, now, to make a fascinating culture for our characters to inhabit, embody, and disrupt. A culture that will both create opportunities for our characters and exert pressures on them. What do our elves value? How do they respond to death—in what specific ways does their culture teach them to experience and

49

display grief? How do they pass on knowledge? How do they fight, and why? What is most scary to them, and what is most taboo? (Hint: Those are the things you will be making them deal with in your exciting story about elves fleeing the super-salamander-dragon through the cold marsh.)

If the marsh-dragons have been changing half the world into swamp over the past centuries, how have our elves responded to the moistening of their home? Do their matriarchs still keep alive some of the old dry-woodland trees, and do the elves grieve at the slow rotting and dying of these trees? What stories do their elders tell, to help the people process what is happening to their land? Do they regard mildew with religious dread? What does *being dry* mean to them? How does *being dry* in an increasingly marshy world shape status and fashion in their culture? Are some of the elves beginning to love the marsh? Does this create tension in the culture between the old and the young, between those who walk dry-footed on rope bridges between the high tree-houses and those who live low by the water and get around by raft or coracle?

CULTURE MEETS CREATURE

The elves' culture and civilization will interact intensely with both the physical conditions for survival in their environment and the marvelous creatures that inhabit that environment. Some of what is most memorable to the reader about the imaginary culture will rise out of that interaction.

Thus, fans remember (and can often recite) the Shai'Hulud prayer of the Fremen in Dune, which the desert people recite whenever they see the passing of a giant sandworm:

> Bless the Maker and His water.
> Bless His coming and His going.
> May His passage cleanse the world.

Sometimes what is unforgettable is not a *giant* piece of the fictional world, but a tiny one. As with the sandworm, so with a rare and tiny blossom that is plucked and treasured by an entire village. So with a stone of black obsidian, a miraculous rock that doesn't appear to belong in this marshy world—how did it get here? One moment that I remember very clearly from Richard Ellis Preston, Jr.'s post-apocalyptic *Romulus Buckle and the City of the Founders*, a novel packed with wonders, is this little scene describing an encounter with the smallest of birds, near the end:

> There were hummingbirds on Catalina, little flitting creatures with blurred wings that appeared at dawn and danced across the snow in flashes of color, of green and blue and crimson. They were one species that had found a way to flourish after the Storming. Max liked watching them; she was an engineer down to her bones, but there was a naturalist's bird's nest in a corner of her heart…
>
> The hummingbirds darted in and out of the long row of funeral pyres, twenty-two in all, poking at the stacks of wood and dead grass, apparently attracted by the kerosene oil that had been poured across them. Their little flicks of color added something ethereal, something eternally alive,

to the dead whose bodies rested atop the pyres, mummy-wrapped in white linen.

"It is said that hummingbirds float free of time," Sabrina said, as she and Buckle arrived at Max's shoulder. "And since they know eternity, they always come to welcome the dead."

Think about that a moment—how much the hummingbirds mean to these people, beyond the brief flash of color. The hummingbird here is a reminder of a world of beauty and safety that predated "the Storming." It is a reminder that the dangerous world the characters inhabit is not all that there is—that there have been beauties in the past and there will be again. This idea of a timeless perspective is reinforced by the way the hummingbird appears to hover in midair, as though it "floats free of time." And, visiting the dead, the hummingbird grants that timeless perspective to those who are grieving for their lost crewmates. The meaning that their culture has assigned to the hummingbird's arrival gives the characters a way to contextualize the suffering and pain of the present within the possibility of a larger story. If the hummingbird can "know eternity," maybe human beings can, too—or at least they can know that such a perspective is possible, that there's more to the world than pain and loss, and always will be.

Exercise 14

Pick an animal. It could be a real animal, or an animal from an SF or fantasy novel. But identify what makes this animal unique and memorable. What might a culture celebrate about it? What lessons might a culture learn from that animal? What might that animal and its habits come to mean to them?

Does your imaginary culture revere the beaver for its building? The albatross for its far traveling? Is your culture one of far travelers? Do they design their ships to mimic the albatross, with wide sails?

Better yet: See if you can find an animal that, to this imaginary culture, appears to defy the way things otherwise work—like that hummingbird that holds still in one spot in the air without falling, as though it is subject to neither gravity nor time nor death. What if there is an animal that lays its eggs inside its own skin, so that the hatching young devour the parent? What does that animal teach your characters' civilization—its moralists and its poets and its adventurers alike—about parenthood? About the duties each person has to the next generation? About when to die, and how to do so with dignity? Select an animal whose features or activities appear supernatural or paradoxical, and explore what that animal might mean to the culture you are creating.

Finally, make sure this animal is also a physical threat to your characters. Like the sandworm of Dune, which is both predator and god to the desert people.

Now, once you have that animal in mind, take a fresh sheet of paper—or open a new file on your word processor—and describe how your imagined people adapt to this animal's presence on this world:

1. List one way in which they have designed their homes as shelter against this predator.

53

2. Name one custom they have developed, unique to their culture, as a response to the threat of this organism on their world.

3. Identify one object they keep in their homes, one prayer they recite, or one story they tell that provides evidence of their reverence—not just their fear—of this organism.

Needless to say, you can conduct the exercise above not only with an animal species but with any other unforgettable "creature" that both inhabits your fictional world and has that striking impact on your imagined culture. Maybe in the case of your story-world, the unforgettable creature is a carnivorous plant, or a self-aware and wandering spacecraft, or a hungry god.

Just as the physical conditions for survival on your world exert pressures on the creatures that inhabit it, those creatures themselves also exert pressures on your characters' home and culture. What we must now discover is how your imaginary people, be they elves or aliens, are adapting their home in response to either the threat or the example of the creatures in their world. How your imaginary culture interacts with the imaginary creatures inhabiting its world is an excellent window into the interior lives of your characters: into what they believe and what they care about.

The questions we are trying to answer through this exploration are: In your characters' civilization, what do people dread most? What do they value most? What do they find most beautiful?

In other words—

What do they hold sacred?

INVENTING IMAGINARY RELIGIONS FOR AN IMAGINARY WORLD

Let's start with religion—because the stories that beat at the hearts of great religions are often the stories that define a culture.

If this were an academic text, I would tell you that religions are best illustrated by the "four C's": *cultus* (the rites and rituals shared by followers of that faith), *creed* (a shared set of beliefs, whether formal or informal), *community* (an institution that transmits knowledge about the faith to the next generation and that often oversees or facilitates the rites), and *codes* (suggestions about what constitutes right behavior or right action). Certainly sketching out what these four are can help you a great deal in designing a religion for your imaginary world.

However, I am going to approach this topic not as a scholar of religions but as a storyteller, because at the heart of every great religion is a compelling story about the human condition. So instead of the four C's, I'm going to ask you to focus on four questions about that religion's story. I am adapting these questions from the work of Stephen Prothero in his study *God is Not One*. (I recommend this book highly for those interested in the subject.) Religions offer stories that answer these four questions:

1. What is unsatisfactory or incomplete (or at risk of being so) about the human condition?
2. What would the ideal human condition look like?

3. How do we get there?
4. Who will show us the way?

For example, in Judaism, what is "wrong" with the human condition is that it is lived in exile—exile from God, from each other, from the holy land. The ideal human condition is a *return*—especially a return to *shalom*, a peace in which the community and each individual in it flourishes. You get there by *tikkun olam*, by repairing the world—and you repair the world by telling the stories of how we got here and by pursuing justice: Tell the story, keep the Law. Who shows us the way? Moses, Maimonides, the scholars of the rabbinical tradition, your own rabbi.

In Buddhism, on the other hand, what's unsatisfactory about the human condition is that we waste it craving what we don't have, or desiring that everything we do have remain permanent and unchanging. But of course everything does change, everything is eventually gone, and our desire that it not be so causes us suffering. If desire is the source of our suffering, then the ideal is *nirvana*—emptying ourselves of the desire for permanence. We get there through meditation, through mindfulness, through compassion (which turns our eyes away from our own desires), and through an array of practices that teach us to accept impermanence—as when Tibetan monks create elaborate and beautiful sand mandalas and then toss them to the wind. Who will show us the way? Depending on the particular branch of Buddhism, a lama, a priest, or a bodhisattva might show us the way.

In the Confucian tradition, what's wrong with the world is social chaos. Confucius wrote his *Analects* after watching a China that tore itself apart. He saw villages burned, saw widespread suffering and violence. The story he told to explain how we can avoid the horrors of social disorder is that the human ideal is for everyone to know fully what their role is and then to perform that role fully. When either of these things does not happen, violence is the ultimate result. How do we get there? Through education, by learning to become a "profound person," understanding and fulfilling our duties to one another and treating each moment as a profound moment. We train ourselves to inhabit our role fully when we treat each moment as sacred—the pouring of tea, the grace with which we walk down a street, the way we greet a neighbor. And we have written texts of ancient sages to show us how.

In Yoruba—the constellation of religious traditions current in the Caribbean and West Africa—what is amiss is that you have forgotten your purpose. Before you were born, you knew what your destiny would be, but in the shock of being born, with that first birthcry, you forgot it. The ideal state is everyone knowing their destiny and fulfilling it. How do you remember what you were meant to do on this world?—You might consult the hundreds of spiritual beings that populate the world, or you might consult your ancestors; *they* haven't forgotten. Divination may be helpful, or a séance, or a ritual dance in which one of the orishas possesses you and gives ecstatic insight. Who can help? There are trained practitioners who can consult the other world for you—or can mentor you.

Notice that each of these stories is profoundly different. They each understand the problem of the human condition very differently, and propose different solutions to it. As storytellers ourselves, we are in a rare position to honor the uniqueness, creativity, and diversity of the world's religious stories. If you want to create imaginary religions for your imaginary world, you need to step away from three intellectual traps. The first trap is to rank religions in their order of superiority, which is a way of failing to understand any of them. The second trap is to treat all religions as having the same goal, as if they are all flavors of ice cream rather than divergent stories about what it means to be human; this, too, is a way of failing to understand any of them. The third trap is to be dismissive of all religions as backwards superstition—which isn't going to be very useful to you either in understanding how they work or in designing some.

The key is to create the story at the heart of the religion, and to understand where that story came from. The Jewish story was written in exile, and so it regards exile as a metaphor for humanity's ailment; Confucius wrote watching a country tear itself apart, so he understand civil strife and lack of social harmony as the ultimate problem. And so on. Each of these stories has an origin point; each is shaped by the conditions of that world in which the religion's first thinkers and doers found themselves.

So if your imaginary world is one that is forever winter, what religion might be created? Do your imaginary people build their story around the necessity of carrying the embers of last night's fire to the next campsite, and then the next, and the next, of not ever letting the fire go out? What would happen if it did? Perhaps in your story-world this becomes both actual, physical practice (carrying the fire) and metaphor (how do each of us carry the fire within our hearts, from one night to the next, from one generation to the next?).

As for the literal fire, who carries it? How are they perceived by the rest of their people? Is it the same person always, or does the task rotate from one person to the next, so that carrying the fire is a shared responsibility among the people? In either case, how would that choice affect how this people establish hierarchy, how they govern themselves, how they understand service and leadership? Oh, and by the way, knowing all of this, you suddenly have the seeds for a number of potential plots. For example:

- A young girl whose task today is to carry the fire loses it or lets it go out, and she must leave the people to go find fire again, alone or with her sisters. (To start developing a plot, ask: What will make her quest difficult?)

- An elder who has carried the fire alone all his life has just witnessed the death of the apprentice he had groomed for the task, and now must find another. (To start developing a plot, ask: What will make his quest difficult?)

And so on.

Once you know the core story of the religion on your invented planet or city or alternate world, you can ask a number of useful, idea-generating follow-up questions:

1. What kind of rituals does this religion require, and who participates in them?

2. What traditions and institutions develop to transmit this religious story to the next generation? In other words, who owns and transmits the people's knowledge and the people's stories? Do these institutions eventually come to act in ways that are no longer compatible with the values displayed in that story?

3. What characters, past or present, in your world exemplify this religion's best impulses? Who is your world's Buddha, its Jesus, its Mahatma Gandhi, its Martin Luther King Jr.?

4. Who is its Torquemada, its Cotton Mather? Who turns this religious story into an excuse for violence, and why?

5. Who wants to reform and revise this religion, and why?

6. What other religions clash with this one, on your imaginary world? How are their stories about the human condition (or the Elven condition, or the Martian condition) different? Even incompatible?

Exercise 15

Imagine a world where the people live hundreds of years. They might understand the 'mortal condition' very differently than we do. Maybe what *they* think is wrong in their lives is ennui: the sadness that comes of watching the world age and die around you and feeling that nothing ultimately matters. (There is the old joke about Tolkien's Middle Earth that the immortal Elves die in the end of one of two causes: a spear thrust, or extreme ennui.) Describe the religion that this culture has developed in order to "solve" ennui.

Further questions: Are there prophets in this imaginary religion? Are there priests? Do they despise each other? (Priests are often agents of the status quo, which prophets threaten to upturn either with new, individual revelations or with demands that the priests be true to the religion's original values and story.) Are there gods? An afterlife? A pre-life? A reincarnation cycle? Upon death, is the deceased eaten by their family so that their knowledge and wisdom is reabsorbed back into the people, and not lost forever? What happens when that culture encounters a second culture that has a taboo against cannibalism? (Anne Rice built her origin story of the vampires around that scenario, in *Queen of the Damned*.)

Maybe there is an afterlife, but it isn't easy to get to, and you need someone at the point of death to show you the way down the last road. Perhaps this is a priest, or a dead loved one, or an angelic being, or even something as unexpected and seemingly absurd as a peppermint-colored squirrel. Perhaps if you have lived a good life and have lived it to the fullest, a peppermint-colored squirrel will appear to you once before your death and then you will know that this squirrel will greet you on the last, violet-strewn road after you draw your last breath. But maybe your character is approaching death and has never seen a peppermint squirrel. If he could only see one—one peppermint-colored emissary from another world—he would know there was a place waiting for him in it. Perhaps, anxious, terrified, your character goes on a quest to find a peppermint squirrel.

Do you see how this can be fun?

When you find your fictional civilization's core religious story, you have found what is most at stake for them, what they most desire and what they most fear.

Exercise 16

I am going to give you answers to two of the four questions, and then I want you, in this exercise, to answer the other two questions. Answer them beautifully or outlandishly, and try to imagine what stories you could spin involving characters who understand their world in this way.

What is amiss in the dwarven condition?

In a word, mortality. Entropy. All things decay. All cities become ruins; all great works of sculpture and craftsmanship eventually crack or crumble or are lost, given enough time. Nothing is permanent.

What would make us whole?

Permanence. Something of beauty that will last the ages. Make something of beauty, and *you* last the ages.

So: you answer these two questions for the dwarves: How do we get there? And: Who will show us the way?

And once you have done this, ask yourself: What characters could I write who might believe this? Or, what characters could I write who might rebel against this belief?

Exercise 17

Create another imaginary religion. This time, I'll give you the answer to the last of the four questions—*Who will show us the way?* Knowing what this culture's sages look like, see if you can answer the first three questions and reverse-engineer their religious story. Come up with something compelling, something striking. This is an imaginary religion after all. No religion sweeps across a globe without a *really* compelling story.

Who will show us the way?
Elliana, the Great Prophet-Singer, who could not speak human words but sang the music of the gods from her throat. She teaches us to hum. She teaches us to hum not only with our throats but with our whole bodies, to hum with perfect joy. She visits you at your deathbed, where only you can see her, and hums with you. She visits you in the womb before you are born. She visits you in the pleasure-surge of your body when you are with your lover.

There. Now, knowing who these characters revere (and perhaps worship), answer the other three questions about this imaginary faith. What is amiss in the human condition? What would make it whole? How do we get there?

And once you have done this, ask yourself: What characters could I write who might believe this? Or, what characters could I write who might rebel against this belief?

THEIR MOST PRIZED VALUE

Here is another route to get at what is most *core* to a culture. Answer the question: What is your fictional civilization's most prized value? And how do their cultural heroes exemplify and demonstrate that value? This will tell you what their stories are—and who the young people in that culture strive to emulate and imitate.

In Homer's *Odyssey*, for example, the most prized value is *metis*: cunning. It shapes everything in that story, everything in how that culture regulates itself and responds to the world. Why does Odysseus earn the favor of Athena, goddess of wisdom? Because of his cunning. Why does he alone, of all his crew, make it back? Because he is willing to defer the fulfillment of his desires. Because he can evade a trap. Because he can plot and plan. Because he can set his warrior-pride aside and wear a disguise. And who is Odysseus's spouse and life-mate? Penelope, whose *metis* matches or exceeds his own. Penelope, cunning and full of tricks and able to use every resource at her disposal to achieve her ends. The culture in this story prizes resourcefulness and intelligence, qualities that in the world of the story are in short supply.

But what if your imaginary culture prizes something else? What if the highest value is *honor*, as in so many tales of Arthurian knights? Or *piety* and *duty*, as in so many tales of Rome? For the kif in C.J. Cherryh's *Chanur* saga, the most prized value is *sfik*: the accumulation of influence. For the Ferengi in Star Trek, the most prized value is *acquisition*.

What would it look like if you wrote a culture whose most prized value was *compassion*? Or *decorum*? Or, conversely, *spontaneity*? How would a culture that values spontaneity above all else choose to structure itself (if "structure" here isn't an oxymoron!)? What would be its institutions? What would its art look like? What would its children be taught? How would people go about seeking a mate? How would funerals be conducted? Et cetera.

Exercise 18

Think of a member of your fictional culture. From *their* perspective, complete the following statements, filling in each of the blanks below:

Before I die, I will _____ at least once.
If I _____, I will have failed at life.
The one thing I must tell my offspring is _____.
At my funeral, I want people to _____.
What I desire most in a mate is _____.
The hero I revere most in the stories of my people once did a thing. This is what the hero did: _____.

If you already know what the 'most prized value' is in this imaginary culture, then look at how your character filled in these blanks, and see how these reflect that value. If the responses don't reflect that value, is there another core value emerging, one that rings more true for this world and the stories you will tell about it, but that you perhaps didn't expect? Or does your character stand apart from their culture?

If you *don't* know yet what the 'most prized value' in this culture is, go hunting for it among the answers your character put in the blanks above. What does your character appear to admire or aspire to? What's most important to them? How do they want to live? These are all important clues, and useful items to know for your story.

HOUSES, AND THE IDEA OF HOME

Architecture may sound to some of you like a dry subject, but bear with me for a moment and I will tell you a secret that is not so secret. It is this: The way we design our homes and our cities reveals nearly everything about us, about how we construct and live in and move through social spaces.

Here's an example from the Historian's Note in my novel *What Our Eyes Have Witnessed*. Consider the importance of windows in this alternate-history, zombie-infested Rome:

> When the dead walked the streets, Romans shut their doors—but the type of refuge one took depended on caste. The patricians on the Palatine Hill lived in vast, one-story villas with no outward-facing windows; all windows looked inward, on a shrine about the hearth and on a garden atrium spacious enough to walk about and take pleasure in. Before the rising of the dead, this lack of outer windows served to prevent the inconvenience of looking at one's neighbor; a high-caste villa (inhabited by a single family) was its own unit, inviolable and inviting no interference in its own governance.

The multistoried and crowded apartment complex one encountered in the slums, known as the insula, was a very different type of shelter. While there were no outward windows on the first story (originally a precaution against thieves), the upper stories had windows looking both inward on the narrow atrium and outward on the streets and the other buildings that loomed near. In the insula, it was impossible to ignore one's neighbors. You could hear them through the wall. You could smell them. You could hear the splash as the next-door tenant tossed his offal into the street. If you stepped to your window, you could see the daily traffic of the Subura, and once the plague began, you could see the dead hunting.

Do you see? Whether your windows face inward to an atrium or outward toward your neighbors can reveal a lot about how you interact with your world and the people in it.

Suppose you create a world of sylvan druids who live inside of titanic trees. What spaces do they carve (or grow) inside those trees? Do they all live in one warren together? Do they have family units? Do they have privacy? What does it mean to live higher in the tree, nearer the leaves? What does it mean to live nearer the roots?

Or maybe your culture lives in tents. How do they orient those tents? Which direction do the doors face, and why? Do they face the way they have come, or the way they are going? Do they face toward (or away from, respectfully) a holy place? What are the tents made from? (Bison? Dragonhide? The skins of their enemies?)? How many people live in a tent? Who tends the fire in the cookpit? Who hunts? Who forages? What might cause someone to be exiled, even temporarily, from the tent? Is there a special white tent to house the diseased?

These are not just *logistical* questions. They aren't even just architectural questions, at least not in a merely technical sense. The question you are exploring when you design a fictional house inhabited by fictional people on a fictional world is: How does this design of a house express a specific idea of home? How does it express and enact the core beliefs and values of the culture—or of the microculture of a specific family?

Every home answers two questions in its own particular way. Those questions are:

1. What does this home shelter people from?
2. What (and who) does this home shelter?

Homes are shaped by both the physical *and* social conditions for survival in your fictional world. Shelter is one of our most basic needs for survival. And every home, from the rock cave in the desert to the spinning orbital pleasure palace, offers a specific response to those survival-level questions: Who is being sheltered? What are they being sheltered from? Different cultures respond to these questions differently. In the case of the Roman villa in my example above, what is being sheltered is the Roman nuclear family, and part of what they are being sheltered *from* is their neighbors.

Here are some productive questions for exploring this further:

1. What does this home shelter people from?

- If home is a place of safety, what are you safe from when you're there? What physical conditions for survival or what creatures have made *this* kind of home necessary? How has this home developed as an adaptation to this fictional world's unique environment? In what ways is this home "safe"?

- What are this home's unique vulnerabilities in your imaginary world, and how do the characters compensate for these? (In Tornado Alley, we build tornado cellars; what innovations does the fictional home in your world require?)

- How does this culture understand the concept of 'home'? What does 'home' feel like to them? What does it mean? Is 'home' a refuge? A hearth? Is 'home' something nomadic, something you carry on your back—and wherever you rest, that is 'home'? Is home "where the heart is," or is home a highly individualized and creative expression of one's heart?

- In this specific culture, what does it feel like to "lose" a home?

2. What (and who) does this home shelter?

- What is the core family unit? How many people live in one home? How many generations?

- What is the central room of the home (what is the home designed "around")?

- How does the design of these homes reinforce certain hierarchies?

- How do these homes shape expectations around privacy?

- In other words—how does this specific kind of home shape the social space and social interactions that happen inside it?

Exercise 19

You know the drill. Here are two different kinds of homes. Your job is to imagine, for each, what kind of culture might produce them and what kind of environment rendered these homes necessary or attractive.

1. First, homes that fly. Fifty people may live together in one flying house, and these houses flock in "cities" of hundreds, which fly swiftly from one place to another, consuming the resources available in that location for a few weeks, then flying on.

2. Second, imagine a culture whose members each live alone in their own house, and this is a house that they grow around them—the way a snail grows the shell on its back. The house encloses them, and they spend decades cultivating and shaping their home.

In each of these two cases, jot down some notes about this culture's religion and its most prized value. What stories would people in this culture tell about their world? What do they fear most? What do they want most? What do they think the purpose of life is? And what does "home" feel like in each of these two cases?

What kind of stories might you write in such a world? What does coming of age look like in that world? What does mating look like? So much conflict in our own world is driven by how we think about home—the need to get a home, the need to protect our home, the fear of losing a home. What conflicts might arise in these two imaginary worlds, where "home" looks so different?

Transportation and accessibility

Here are a few related questions that almost no one thinks about—but that could help you develop some creative and detailed worlds if you did:

- How does this culture handle accessibility? When members of the society are disabled, how is their mobility addressed?
- What do this culture's modes of transportation from one place to another reveal about the way people in this fictional civilization look at their world and their roles in it?

For example, in *The Left Hand of Darkness*, people on the planet Winter have automobiles, but they never travel above 25 miles per hour. It would never occur to them to do so. There is no reason on Winter to rush from one location to another. This lack of haste offers clues to how they live differently and understand their duties and roles on Winter differently than we do in, say, the United States or Canada. Even on our own earth, various cultures approach transportation differently. For example, the

Incas probably knew of the wheel, but they never put the wheel to use; on the terraced steps of the high Andes, the wheel would have been wildly impractical.

Conversely, what does transportation look like for those who can *only* use wheels? In David Brin's *Brightness Reef*, he imagines an alien species that has been genetically engineered for rapid speed on suborbital platforms—in space. The g'Keks have wheels instead of limbs, and when a secret colony of g'Keks joins five other species on a hidden world, accommodations are made for their mobility. This world's cities have wide sidewalks and wheel-accessible doors and ramps. There is even one city—which serves as a home for the g'Keks—that is *all* sidewalks and wide, paved loops.

Our own culture tends toward ignoring those with physical disabilities and their needs, quietly excluding them from our communal home. But suppose your imaginary culture is one in which the blind or the lame or the deaf endure no stigma; they might hold positions of honor as easily as the sighted, the walkers, and the hearing do. How might such a civilization design its homes and its cities differently, more inclusively, than we do? What would a city look like that didn't rely on visual signs to get its traffic from one place to another? What would a home look like that was not only modified but designed from the start for a person in a wheelchair? What if your imagined world is one in which blindness is normative, and nothing in the world has been designed for sighted people? What difficulties might a sighted character encounter? Maybe there is no lighting at night or inside of buildings, for their fellow citizens have no need of it.

Researching and answering these questions could lead you to create an interesting house, an interesting city, and an interesting culture different from any that the reader knows. And maybe encountering that civilization might even inspire readers to create something innovative and beautiful one day—the way Arthur C. Clarke inspired satellites and the way *Star Trek* inspired cell phones. I haven't talked about it much in this book, but creating an imaginary world is a powerful act. When you create an unforgettable world, you create something whose details readers might want to avoid or replicate, depending on the world. We entertainers and storytellers sing for our supper and hope to amuse, thrill, or delight, but sometimes we also manage (perhaps unexpectedly) to inspire the building of a cathedral, or the invention of a computer, or a heroic act. You never know.

So if your fantasy or science fiction novel permits it, consider writing one detail into your world that is amazing and helpful.

Something we have never seen before.

Something we really ought to have, but don't.

Yet.

RUINS AND RELICS OF THE PAST

Even as your body carries the marks of your history—scars of past injuries or tattoos that tell parts of your story to yourself—so the landscape carries marks of the past, each of which has a story. Those marks and ruins may tell the story (the history) of the characters' home and their people...or even the story of a lost, half-remembered home.

We have been talking about the alien civilization you are writing as though it exists in a kind of timeless present, but the reality is that it has a past that will continually burst up into that present, a past that is never rendered entirely invisible. What ruins or monuments of that past might your characters encounter either near their home (as they go about their daily lives) or on their journeys? Who put those artifacts there, and have they been abandoned? Are they celebrated or half-forgotten? Put on your archaeologist's fedora and think about:

- Public monuments that are taken care of and revered, that tell important stories of the past.
- Portable relics of a revered past that the characters might keep or carry with them.
- Overgrown roads, collapsed bridges, shattered arches, and weatherworn statues left behind by a past empire or occupying state.
- Ruins of such antiquity that their purpose is now a mystery, and your characters have devised their own theories for why these majestic and enigmatic structures were created and what purposes they once served.

Let's take a quick glance at some of the worldbuilding possibilities presented by each of these.

Public monuments

Coming up with a public monument can tell you not only about the historical events that have shaped your imaginary civilization, but also a great deal about what their values are, who their heroes are, and whose history they are interested in telling. Monuments tell people who to emulate—and who has power. For example, a statue of a famous woman who gave up fame and queenship to retreat into the country to raise seven children could send a message to other women in this imaginary society that they are expected to be mothers (and only mothers), and not leaders. Similarly, many Confederate statues in our own United States were erected during the period of the Jim Crow laws as an explicit message to black citizens, so that even today in some cities African American children have to walk past statues of slave-owners on their way to school and remember what this society believes their place in it is.

Monuments can reveal what is heroic in a society but also what is cruel. You might see plaques commemorating those who died in atrocities, like the plaque in the Jewish Quarter in Venice. Monuments can also reveal what a society fears. Consider the sculpture of Roma that stood for centuries in the Forum of ancient Rome. This marble statue of a woman was always provided with a cloth gag, because in Rome there was a popular legend that one day the statue of Roma would speak the true name of the city, and on that day the city would fall. Consider how that statue, carefully rendered voiceless, reveals how Rome feared women's speech—and how it hints at the misogyny of some of the solutions Rome found for addressing that fear. If a statue of a woman must be kept gagged, what does Rome believe about the need to silence living women?

Exercise 20

Pick something that your imaginary civilization fears deeply. Design a statue, monument, or other physical memorial that represents symbolically the need to face, subdue, or overcome what is feared. Do this twice. The first time, come up with a monument that offers an unhealthy or abusive message, like the gagged statue of Roma. The second time, come up with a statue or monument that symbolizes a healthier approach to meeting what this civilization fears. What does each version of the monument reveal about this imaginary culture?

Relics

A related line of inquiry is to investigate what *relics* this culture holds dear. Does your character carry with her a fingerbone of a long-dead prophet or saint? An urn containing the ash of a legendary cleric? A knife or locket that was the property of a great-great-grandmother? What value, sentimental or magical, do these relics confer? How are these relics preserved and kept and passed on? Has your main character, roguishly, *stolen* a relic that they now hold dear? All this can offer some clues about what stories and heroes are important to this culture, and about the specific ways in which your characters see themselves connected to the past.

Come up with the most unique and surprising relic you can think of. What if that relic is the overriding detail that makes this imaginary civilization unforgettable? Maybe this culture keeps all of its stillborn babies preserved perfectly in transparent containers. Far from a morbid motive, maybe the mothers in this culture pickle the dead children because they loved them so much, and because they want them to stay a part of the people. Consider: Where are these containers kept? In a temple? In the houses? Maybe one preserved infant is stolen. Who would steal it, and why? What trauma would that cause the parents, or others in the society? What might they do to get it back? The story of chasing a dead baby across an alien landscape might sound bizarre, but stranger things have happened in science fiction and fantasy, and a skilled storyteller could write characters into that story whom we would laugh with and cry for. We might not keep *our* stillborn infants in transparent containers, but if we did, if this was how we honored lives we hoped for that were never lived, if this was central to how we understood family, we would probably move heaven and hell to keep those containers safe.

Maybe this isn't a story of pursuit and recovery. Maybe it is a story of invasion, a story of cultures clashing, a story of desperate resistance. Maybe the invaders are about to loot or destroy the House of the Neverborn, and your main character stands in the doorway to stop them. We know she can't stop an entire army. We know they will get through. But not without a fight. And we are breathless, reading of her battle. We weep with her when the fight is lost. And with her, we vow revenge. With her, maybe we cry with joy when, in the ruins of the next day, one of the transparent containers is found unexpectedly intact in the rubble. One of them is safe. She cradles it in her arms, and her tears mist the glass. The House wasn't completely, entirely destroyed after all, and neither will her people be. The resistance will continue. And we, the readers, will keep turning the pages. Where does the main character send that baby-relic? Where does she keep it? How does it become the symbol of the resistance?

Now you do it:

Exercise 21

Come up with:

- A kind of relic that might surprise and startle the reader.
- A reason that explains why that relic exists and why that relic is important to the main character.
- What would it mean to the main character if the relic was lost or destroyed?
- Two ways in which a plotline might hinge on this relic.

Neglected ruins

What monuments, roads, statues, or monasteries have been left in ill-repair and ruin, in your imaginary world? Whose stories does this civilization wish to forget? Are the ruined monuments those of a conquered or exterminated people? Or those of past conquerors, since ousted? The people whose monuments these were—are their descendants around? If so, what names do they have for these ruins? Are these different from the names that are in more popular use? Do these descendants visit the ruins? Do those who are not descendants visit the ruins, too? As tourists? Is a local ruined castle a favorite spot for lovers' trysts? Do the lovers etch their names in the old, mossy stones? Do they chip off pieces to take back with them? How do the descendants of the castle's original builders and occupants feel about this?

Here is something else to think about: One of the reasons that neglected, decaying ruins are so compelling is that their existence calls into question the permanence of our own homes. These *past* homes did not last; why should we think ours will, either? On the other hand, those past homes have left traces behind; ours might, too. Your characters might approach ruins with a complexity of emotions. Remember Percy Shelley's poem "Ozymandias":

> I met a traveller from an antique land,
> Who said—"Two vast and trunkless legs of stone
> Stand in the desert. . . . Near them, on the sand,
> Half sunk a shattered visage lies, whose frown,
> And wrinkled lip, and sneer of cold command,
> Tell that its sculptor well those passions read
> Which yet survive, stamped on these lifeless things,
> The hand that mocked them, and the heart that fed;
> And on the pedestal, these words appear:
> My name is Ozymandias, King of Kings;
> Look on my Works, ye Mighty, and despair!
> Nothing beside remains. Round the decay
> Of that colossal Wreck, boundless and bare
> The lone and level sands stretch far away."

In the half-imagined desert world of this poem, two stone legs and an inscription are all that remain not only of the sculpture but of an entire civilization. Look on my works, ye mighty, and despair: That past civilization thought itself mighty and conquering and immortal. But it was not. The traveler who comes upon that inscription amid a sea of dunes might receive the shock of realizing their own home is equally transient. Ruins can be both wondrous and unsettling.

The older ruins that have no names

What was Stonehenge? Was it a meeting place? A house of worship? A tomb? A place for wizards to watch the stars? There are nearly as many theories as there are archaeologists. The original meaning of the ruin has been lost to time, though we keep finding clues and evidence that help us sort through the prevailing theories. Since there are so many possibilities, what meaning and significance we attach to Stonehenge today often reveals more about ourselves—our own contemporary cultures and values—than about the original builders of Stonehenge.

Maybe there are ruins in your fictional world that offer similar mysteries. Maybe there is a face carved into the side of a mountain—much larger than Rushmore—but nobody knows whose face it was. Some people think the face looks stern and even a little cruel; others merely think the face is strong and stoic.

Maybe there are paintings on a cave wall of people fighting (or hunting, or fleeing, or *riding*) mysterious beasts that have never been seen, whose bones have never been found. Surely they are mythical. Maybe these beasts make a startling reappearance in the contemporary present, in your story.

Maybe there is a ruined temple, and all the walls are painted with images of screaming faces. Maybe there is grove of marble trees that was "planted" three thousand years ago, and no one knows why that grove is there or what it means—only that is lovely, and out of the way, and quiet.

Are there structures that have been left throughout the galaxy by a species of explorers that is now a billion years extinct—like the massive artifacts left behind in Jack McDevitt's *The Engines of God*? Is there writing on these structures that no one can read? Perhaps technology that no one knows how to access?

Consider: What scenes might take place in such abandoned locales? What might these locations come to mean to your characters? Do the ruins mean something to your main character that is very different from what they appear to mean to everyone else?

Exercise 22

Imagine a fantasy world set five centuries in our future. The ruins of our own cities and monuments are still visible beneath layers of toxic vegetation. The civilization in this story has little memory of us. How do they interpret the ruins we have left behind? Which ruins do they avoid, and why? Which do they revere?

Come up with a story or a theory that this imagined civilization has about each of the following:

1. The St. Louis arch.
2. The Washington monument, which is nearly the only part of Washington, D.C. still standing.
3. A ruined Interstate, where trees grow out of the hulks of cars that have rusted almost entirely away.
4. The Statue of Liberty.
5. A compact disc (CD) that one of the characters finds in the wood.

What do these mysterious ruins *mean* to the culture in this imaginary future world? When you find this out, consider how this information might aid you in writing the perspective of a member in that far-future culture.

To explore this more deeply, consider pursuing this exercise from the perspectives of three different characters:

A. First, from the perspective of an elder in this culture, who transmits the tribe's stories of the past to the next generation. The elder will describe the ruin and its story in ways that communicate beliefs and practices they wish the tribe to uphold. Perhaps to the elder, the ruin is a warning—but of what?

B. Next, describe an archaeologist's encounter with the ruin. How would this individual interpret these traces of a forgotten past? What theories would they try to affirm or deny when they discover the ruin? What other items do they discover nearby that might shed light on—or complicate—the ruin's meaning to them? How does the ruin deepen or shake up the archaeologist's understanding of their world?

C. Finally, describe the ruin through young eyes. In this case, either a spurned lover who has fled their mate and is sleeping by the ruin tonight—or a youth fleeing an arranged marriage and using the ruin as a hiding place. What does this young person notice about the ruin? If they've seen it before, what do they now notice for the first time, in the night, as they take refuge there? How do the recent events of the youth's life affect how they interpret the ruin—or, vice versa, how does the experience of hiding by or in this ruin help them understand what has just happened to them differently?

TECHNOLOGY & MAGIC

The tools and tech that are available to us shape our lives and the way we think and interact with others, often in more fundamental ways than we realize. Consider how different social interaction has become, now that many of us carry a small computer in our pocket. Or consider how the invention of electric lighting not only made lighting safer but changed the way we think about *day* and *night*— changed sleeping habits and patterns, changed expectations around productivity, hobbies, and social life. In an agrarian society, we rose with the sun and went to bed when the stars came out. That is not the case in a post-industrial, urban, electric society. Think of all the social connections, friendships, study, and love affairs that are carried out under electric lighting at night. Think about the impact of light pollution—that in many parts of the United States, you see few if any stars when you look up at the night sky. Past cultures told elaborate stories about that blaze of the Milky Way, invented astrologies, conceived of the billion lighted cities of heaven, or even yearned to visit those distant stars.

Consider how advances in medicine change not only our lifespan but also how we think about our bodies. Or how the ability to call up information on Google makes memory and mental recall seem at times redundant. Past cultures committed entire books to memory as a survival tactic, but they could never have imagined the access to information we now have.

Where I am going with this is: When you decide on a level of technology or when you invent a technological or magical system for your fantasy or science fiction world, you are inventing more than just a set of tools or a list of spells and abilities. You are shaping how your fictional civilization understands itself. We are tool users, but the tools use us, too: they shape us as we shape them. Technology is both an expression *of* the characters' culture and a window *into* it.

Let's take a closer look.

How does our idea of home shape our tools?

Our technology develops out of the same needs that are expressed in our homes and shelters; we design tools that enact our idea of home. For example, in the United States, the same conditions that have shaped our single-family houses shape the technologies we prioritize and develop and buy: our desire for immediate access to both resources and entertainment, our desire for privacy and autonomy, and—paradoxically—our longing to be more connected with each other without sacrificing our autonomy. Is it any wonder that these desires get expressed technologically in social media apps on smartphones we carry in our pockets and purses?

So first, consider how your fictional culture's technologies (or magic, for that matter) are extensions of their ideas of home and community.

How do our tools shape us?

Next, once you know how your fictional culture has shaped its technology or magical system (and why), here are three questions you can ask to explore how those tools or spells then shape their users:

1. How does the technology/magic shape your characters' perceptions?
2. Is the technology/magic considered "natural" or "unnatural?"
3. What devices does your character carry?

Let's take a brief look at each of these questions and its implications for your worldbuilding and your story.

1. How does the technology/magic shape your characters' perceptions?

If people in your world have cloning, then consider how this shapes the way they understand identity, family, and mortality. If people in your world commit a thousand spells to memory, how does this change the way they train their memories and their minds generally? Do they have eidetic or photographic memories? Are they able to instantly recall a recent conversation in all of its detail? How might this shape the way they conduct romantic relationships, the way they conduct business, the way they attempt to deceive each other, the way they transmit knowledge from one generation to the next? If memorization is the most critical survival skill, do they even have books? If they do, does this make magic more or less difficult to remember and perform?

And how does the technology or the magic alter how this civilization sees its world? When we can fly from one continent to another overnight, we think about the size of the world and the distance between its peoples differently. If your mages can open portals for instantaneous teleportation from one site to another, how does that change the way they understand the size of their world? Do your mages describe the planet as a single house with endless rooms? Is traveling to another continent—or even another planet, or another galaxy, or another dimension— a matter of stepping from one room to the next? If not *all* of your characters are mages, how might you illustrate and play with the differences in how the mages see the world, versus how everyone else sees their world?

2. Is the technology/magic considered natural or unnatural?

Another way that you can discover (and uncover, for your readers) details about your world is to explore whether the technologies and magical systems that exist in it are considered natural or unnatural, and by whom. We all know the trope of the villagers with the pitchforks who are prepared to burn the witch because her magic is unnatural and scary to them, but there are more subtle things you can do, too.

For example, consider how different members of different generations react to social media in our own culture. To some, this technology appears deeply unnatural or unhealthy; they blame it for leaving people disconnected with each other. To others, this technology appears deeply natural and healthy; they praise it for connecting people all over the world and for permitting the formation of social networks and long-term friendships for those individuals who, for medical or other reasons, had few such opportunities prior to this technology. Do Facebook and Twitter hasten the decay of civilization, or do they improve it? It is up to the characters in our story—each of us—to figure that out.

In Margaret Weis and Tracy Hickman's *Death Gate Cycle*, most societies on the various worlds are well-acquainted with magic. Most magics are "natural," though few can use them or use them well. Mages exert their will to change something in the world around them. However, in the novels there are two races—Patryns and Sartan—whose magic is overwhelming. These mages are capable of feats the others don't even understand. Their "unnatural" magic works according to an entirely different system of rules. The Patryns cast spells not by exerting their will on some natural object, but by looking at the thousands of things that could possibly happen in a given moment, and choosing one that *will* happen. Then they sing the runes, and it does. The more improbable the event they summon into existence, the more effort it requires. Nearly anything is *possible*, of course; a dragon could swoop through the window and burn your opponent to a crisp. It's not *likely*, but it's *possible*. And if a Patryn can imagine it, she can cast the spell to make it happen. This magic is rather a shock to the others who live in these worlds. It makes the Patryns and Sartan seem like gods—a circumstance that these two races abuse horribly.

In the same universe, there are also magics— technologies—that the Patryns and Sartan themselves regard as "unnatural" and abhorrent. One is necromancy, because in order for necromancy to work—in order for you to breathe life into a dead corpse—a life must be taken from somewhere else, from a living body. A life for a life. The more corpses raised, the more people inexplicably die untimely deaths somewhere else. The characters can see how the magic works; they can understand the system. But a lot of conflict in the story proceeds from their horror at the "unnaturalness" of this technology and over the question of whether or not to wield it.

3. What devices does your character carry?

Earlier, we discussed *relics* your character might carry on their person. But what about *tools*? (A device can, of course, also be both.) Eyeglasses or spectacles. A cell phone. A *Star Trek* tricorder. A gun. A blade. A quill and inkwell. A magic wand. What technologies do your characters carry on—or *in*—their bodies? How does this shape their habits and the way they move through the story you are writing?

In my *Tyrannosaur* stories, the young athletes who are trained to compete on tyrannosaur-back aboard orbital colosseums carry inside their bodies billions of nanites, microscopic machines that are continually modifying their bodies—shaping them for strength and speed, healing injuries swiftly, and forcing their bodies into whatever form pleases the cameras and the crowds. Nyota Madaki, the protagonist of my forthcoming novel *Nyota's Tyrannosaur*, is always aware of the presence of these nanites inside her:

> They are my torment and my necessity. I could starve after an energy burn like last night's, yet the nanites will keep me moving and alive, a tyrannosaur rider rather than tyrannosaur food…

Nyota will dare physical feats that risk catastrophic injury because she knows the nanites will modify her even as she leaps, heal her even as she falls. But magic always comes at a cost, and that can often be true of technology as well. When Nyota looks in a mirror, she does not recognize her own body. It changes too often. Displaced within her own body and driven by the rigors of a physical and mental training regime that requires her to regard others as competitors, not companions, she suffers a terrible solitude that the story I have placed her in will attempt to heal:

> I am myself an ecosystem of microscopic, semisentient machines, yet I stand here alone. Truly alone.

Another example. In my novel *Strangers in the Land,* the middle-aged Bronze Age prophetess Devora suffers conflicted feelings about the iron sword concealed in her tent—a weapon that in a world of bronze seems nearly like magic. When she goes out from her tent to safeguard her people from thousands of ravenous dead, she takes up the blade, but with distaste. It becomes one of her most important tools (though not the only one), but she cannot wield it without facing the memory of infected loved ones she had to put out of their misery in the past. Taking up that blade, she assumes the responsibility of deciding when people must die. Wearing this device at her side and being ready to use it also entails a commitment to rapid decision and immediate action, which is unsettling to a character who normally spends her days deliberating over legal cases and thinking matters over with care:

> "I will name you Mishpat," she whispered to the blade, "the Judgment. That will help us both remember what you are and what you are not." A judgment on the dead. A judgment on her. The swift cut of decision, severing what limbs must be severed from the body of the People so that the rest of the body might thrive and not decay.

Think of the devices *your* character might carry, in the imaginary world you're creating. How do these devices change not only what your character is capable of, but what they are willing to do, what they want to do? What costs do their spells or tools exact from them? And what might be the cost of losing a tool? When you know these things, this will help you boost the drama and tension in your story, because you will have new clues about what is at stake for the characters in tense scenes and scenes of conflict.

Spartan warriors were told to come back "with their shield or on it"—because a warrior fleeing a battle and abandoning his fellow soldiers would have to cast aside the heavy shield he carried. A soldier who appeared back in Sparta without a shield was a deserter. But the body of a soldier slain in combat might be carried home *on* his shield. That shield is thus both a survival tool and a symbol of the soldier's honor and courage. What a horror it would be to your Spartan character if his shield were lost over the side of the ship during a storm! Or what if your character is myopic—as I am—and relies heavily on her spectacles? What if she travels to a planet, or a century, or a dimension where spectacles and the materials to make them don't exist? What if her glasses crack while she is there?

Related to that: How do your characters take care of their devices? Harry Dresden, the Chicago wizard in Jim Butcher's *Dresden Files*, spends time at a punching bag during some of the novels—not to be buff or ready to box, necessarily, but because the power-rings on his fingers require all that movement in order to store up the kinetic energy that will allow him to release a blast of concussive force from them during battle later.

If your character carries a beloved book in their pocket at all times—perhaps a book through which they interpret everything they discover and into whose margins they scribble everything they want to remember, like the battered copy of the *Histories* of Herodotus in *The English Patient*—then how do they care for this book? If it has a cover of old leather, do they also carry some oil with them? Do we see them on their journeys awake late at night, applying the oil by moonlight or a fire's last embers, both to prevent dry rot and to allow them time to meditate on the events of the day?

You get the idea. Identify what the tools or magical devices your characters carry with them mean—what they mean, personally, to that character, and what they mean to the culture. In a good story, they will often mean a great deal to both. Luke Skywalker's lightsaber in the first *Star Wars* movie is, on the one hand, a legacy from his unknown father and a symbol of freedom, heroism, and a larger future ahead of him—and it is also, to the civilization into which he is about to step, a symbol of a better time, a visible promise of justice and of championship for the oppressed.

Exercise 23

Back to the elves fleeing their dragon. What technologies are available to help them fight or evade their pursuer, and what do those technologies cost? Consider four scenarios:

1. The ability to turn invisible—but blood must be shed in order for this to happen.

2. A bow whose arrows will never miss their target—but it can only be wielded by one who hates taking life.

3. The ability to weave nets with slender threads that almost can't be seen from the air. These might be used to entrap a marauding dragon, but the threads can only be spun from (in version 3a) a rare plant deep in the swamp and dangerous to obtain, or (in version 3b) the hair of an unfaithful lover.

4. Ray guns. Why not! Maybe *these* elves crash-landed their spaceship in the dragon's marsh. And they have ray guns. But the power-packs are depleted and, as this planet is fiercely cold, the elves have been using them up starting fires to keep warm. They will have only a few shots.

Now for the imaginative play: What stories might you tell in each of these cases? What does each technology or magic suggest about the elves' culture, and how can you, as the author, use that information in the story? What character might make a good protagonist, in each scenario? How will the protagonist surmount the obstacles to the use of these tools or magics? And—for the sake of suspense and entertainment—how difficult can you make it for them?

LOST IN TRANSLATION

We just spoke about technology. Now let's talk about our *oldest* technology: language. Even in our own world, the same devices can have quite different names in different cultures—which in turn leads to different ways of thinking about how to integrate these tools into our lives. For example, the machine on which I am typing this manuscript is called a *computer* in English—a machine that computes, that calculates, that solves problems. In French, the same machine is *l'ordinateur*, a device that organizes and provides order. The difference is subtle, but if you really think about it—pretty momentous. Or, even within the same language, think about how a different thing comes into your mind depending on whether you say *rocket*, *shuttle*, or *starship*.

What about a *sword*? The English word *sword* simply comes from an adjective meaning "sharp." The Hebrew word *chereb* originally meant "drought"; when you thrust a blade through a person, their blood pours out and there is a drought of blood inside their body. The blood loss has an effect on them as destructive and devastating as the effect of a drought on the land. The Latin word *gladius* means "a breaker" or "a beater": literally a tool for beating the crap out of the people you're trying to subjugate. A tool of Empire.

The different stories contained inside the names of things offer a lot of opportunity for things to be lost in translation. Think about the way people in our own culture often talk about "truth," as though it is a synonym for "fact." Fact comes from the Latin *factum est*: "it happened." And the Latin word that we translate as "truth" in English is *veritas*: that which is sure, that which can be verified. But the English word "truth" is just a modern spelling of *troth*, a promise we trust in. We still keep that meaning today in the word "betrothed." And the Greek word for truth that one finds coined in the New Testament is another thing altogether: *aletheia*, "unforgetting." In Greek myth and lore, the dead drink from the river *lethe* ("forgetting") and lose all memory of their mortal lives and of everything that mattered to them. *Aletheia* is the daily act of *un*forgetting the promises that matter to you. In Greek, truth is an activity.

Now, you don't need to be a philologist to write a fantasy or a science fiction world. You don't even need to invent a language. But one window into your imagined civilization that can be very helpful is to examine the names of things, and what stories those names recall. And not just species and towers and starships. What are the specific names for the core values and the abstract concepts that matter to your fictional people? What is the word they use for *childhood*, and what does that word imply about the fictional culture? What is their word for *peace*? Do they even have a word for war, or do they have seven such words that all mean quite different things to them? What does their word for *justice* mean? And—of course— what is *home* called? How does this culture describe their idea of home? What word is used for 'house' in your fictional culture, and what does that word mean?

If you are writing a story involving multiple characters from multiple cultures, what opportunities for misunderstanding (or, conversely, for sudden and well-timed epiphany) are made possible by these differences in what things are called? There are plenty of examples of this in our own history—including, famously, the mistranslation of *mokusatsu*, whereby the Japanese Prime Minister's remark of "no comment" was misinterpreted as meaning "I am ignoring this ultimatum or treating it with silent contempt." That error in translation—fueled by prevailing stereotypes about the Japanese—may have led to the dropping of the atomic bomb on Hiroshima. Similarly, either the unwillingness or the inability to translate a concept effectively from one culture to another can lead to grave consequences in your imagined world and its history.

But while language can shape the affairs of nations, let's also consider how the names we give things can shape a single life and the story of a single person. For example, consider: *What is your character's profession or vocation, and what is the name for that vocation?* Names matter. Two centuries ago, there was significant pushback against the popular adoption of the word "scientist." Though today many researchers claim that term proudly, at the time that it was originally proposed, many considered it an offensive term. Many researchers preferred to be called *natural philosophers*, because they associated "scientist" with "technician," and they wanted to emphasize that they were concerned not only with how things work but with what it means that things work in that way.

Try this:

Exercise 24

Imagine two versions of a character. In both cases, the character carries messages from city to city by flying across vast chasms of air using artificial wings strapped to their arms and back. In the first version of this story, the character's vocation is that of an *unchained*, one no longer shackled by gravity. For your character who is one of the *unchained*, come up with answers to these questions:

- What kind of school do the *unchained* go to? What is the name or term for that kind of school, and what does it mean? How is an *unchained* trained, and by whom? What did your character have to do to graduate at the top of their class?
- What role models and heroes do the *unchained* look to? What values do these heroes, these past examples of the *unchained*, teach your character? What does your character hope to live up to?

- What is the worst thing that could ever happen to an *unchained*? What would mean total failure to your character? (Hint: Find this out, and you have a story…)

Exercise 25

Now imagine a second story. The physical logistics of the character's vocation are similar: gliding from city to city on artificial wings to deliver messages. But this time, the character is a *voice*. That is their vocation: being a *voice*. How does this shape the character's education, values, goals, fears, and the way they carry out their work, differently than in the first story? Answer the same questions that you did in Exercise 24:

- What kind of school does a *voice* go to? What is the name or term for that kind of school, and what does it mean? How is a *voice* trained, and by whom? What did your character have to do to graduate at the top of their class?
- What role models and heroes does a *voice* look to? What values do these heroes, these past examples of the *voice*, teach your character? What does your character hope to live up to?
- What is the worst thing that could ever happen to a *voice*? What would mean total failure to your character? (Hint: Find this out, and you have a story…)

Maybe, in doing this exercise, you decided that the worst thing that could ever happen to an *unchained* would be to fall from the sky. Or maybe instead, the worst thing was to be caged. But maybe the worst thing that could happen to a *voice* is to be silenced. In that imaginary world, what situation might lead to your character having their vocal cords cut, or to the threat or possibility that this could happen? Or maybe the worst thing that could happen to a *voice* is to be misheard. Or to stumble and misspeak a message. Or maybe a *voice* is trained to speak only the words they are given, and they must be silent except when delivering that message, and the greatest crime is to speak words of their own. Do you see how each of these different possibilities opens up different conflicts, different stories you could tell? And how even the choice of what you name a character's job—and thus also what you name the tools of their profession, what you name the kind of journey they undertake, etc.—could provide you and the reader with windows into different worlds and could prompt the telling of very different stories? Go experiment with that.

RITES OF PASSAGE

In Exercises 24-25, I asked how your character graduates from flight school. We might also ask how characters in your imaginary civilization handle each of their most important transitions. Rites of passage mediate who gets welcomed into the home and into the tribe, and these rites govern the transition from one home to the next. Thus the custom of a groom carrying the bride across the threshold into the new home; the housewarming party to celebrate the purchase of a first home; the funeral and the lowering of the casket to commemorate the transition from an earthly home to whatever the next home after might be.

Rites of passage make the crossing of the threshold into the new home (whether literal or figurative) meaningful, and they provide an occasion for the community to affirm the status and inclusion of the person who is "passing" to the next home and the next stage of life. In other words, rites of passage are both a way in which a community confirms who receives shelter in their homes and an opportunity to change the roles of those living in the home. *Coming of age*, for example, changes the equation of who is providing shelter and who is receiving it.

So ask of your imaginary culture questions like these:

- What are the customs attending a birth? How does a parent prepare? How is an infant welcomed into the world?
- What is the rite that accompanies passage from childhood to adulthood?
- How do members of your culture think and talk about the first time they mate?
- How does your imagined culture handle each major life transition?
- Which life transitions are regarded as *most* meaningful in this culture?

For example, there could be major transitions that don't (or rarely) exist in our own culture, but may be more momentous than marriage or home-buying in your imagined civilization. What about an oath of fealty? What would that oath mean to the one swearing it and the one hearing it, and what ritual would accompany such an occasion? The Anglo-Saxon kings of early medieval

England would slip a ring on the finger of their vassal, a gift that carried it with a promise of a seat at the monarch's table (a place in the monarch's home) for the vassal and for every descendant who would show up wearing that ring. It is a custom that Tolkien's Dark Lord Sauron perverts for malevolent purposes (handing out rings that enslave the wearer more than they convey benefits), and that has inspired our own modern exchange of wedding rings.

You might imagine a society in which a monarch who is accepting an oath of fealty brands a rune on the brow of the one swearing the oath. Should the oath ever be broken, the rune will burn with the heat of a sun and kill the traitor. You can imagine what stories of reckless rebellion and reckless loyalty might be played out on such a world.

Or perhaps oaths of fealty are sealed with acts of sex. What would *that* imply about how your fictional culture views sex, or about how they view loyalty? What is the sex act, in this case, about? Mutually shared vulnerability? The mutual giving of pleasure and security? You're the author; you'll have to determine that.

What about the adoption of children? How is that transition handled in the life of the parent(s) and the life of the child? What does it mean in a civilization where infertility is common? Or where certain religious orders are not permitted to bear children but are expected to foster them?

What about a funeral? How does this culture say goodbye?

Think about all of the big "first" times and think about the important "last" times in your character's life. What most rites of passage have in common is that:

- They enact a journey between homes (a crossing between two states).
- Some specific, ritual act with a physical, tangible object conveys that the crossing has been made.
- There are participants, officiant(s), and witnesses.

The journey

The bride's walk down the aisle, the walk in cap and gown to receive the diploma, the lowering of the casket into the ground, the knight's vigil at the chapel followed by the walk to kneel at the monarch's feet: these are all symbolic journeys that make the transition visible to all present.

The ritual act

The dubbing with the sword, the ring placed on the finger, the kiss, the first shovelful of earth, the ribbon-cutting: these are all actions that convey that the crossing has occurred.

The participants

Who is present is also important: there is often a religious officiant, the persons involved in the transition, and witnesses. Determining who officiates and why (a parent? A priest? An elder?), and who can be included as witnesses and why they are there, can tell you a lot about your imaginary culture. To answer this question, remember that a rite of passage is about a transition between two homes (again, either literally or figuratively). So go back to this fictional culture's idea of home. Who has authority over the home—either the individual home or the communal? This will provide hints as to who the officiants might be.

Once you see how these rites work and why, the final question to ask is: Who is excluded from the right to have these rites? Who is *not* assured a place in the next home, or can achieve such assurance only with difficulty?

Who cannot be married?

Who cannot come of age?

Who cannot be buried in consecrated ground?

And, in your world, in your story, who will transgress these restrictions?

In my novel *No Lasting Burial*, the boy Koach is denied his rite of passage to adulthood because the village will not accept him. He has a withered arm, and they fear this difference. In the story, Koach must find his own crossing, and a community and home that will accept him.

In *Strangers in the Land*, Devora the prophet is the elder who sings the Words of Going at each burial beneath a cairn of stones. All her adult life, she has blamed another tribe for the woes that have befallen her people. But in this novel, she adopts a young woman from that other tribe as the daughter of her heart. And when that young woman dies an untimely death, Devora shocks everyone by singing the Words of Going at her grave:

> Devora worked the men hard, raising Hurriya's cairn. She made it the highest one in that line of silent promises to the dead. When Laban lifted the last stone, it clacked into

place nearly level with his head. The other cairns were already done, and only a few men remained there to see if the *navi* needed help. The other men had left quickly, not wanting to spend longer than they must in the presence of the dead.

"Go," Devora whispered. "All of you."

Laban hesitated, one hand resting on the top of the cairn. "She was not of the People," he said.

"She is of my tribe," Devora said softly. "I accept her as one of my tribe. Please go."

Laban looked at her another moment, then turned without a word and began walking away through the dead field.

Devora leaned on the cairn, her eyes cold as a winter sea. Then she lifted her voice. Though hoarse, she sang with such beauty that men raising tents in the field stopped and stood still, turning to face the cairn and the *navi* beside it.

As the darkness fell, Devora sang her farewell to a woman of her People.

What rites of passage do is convey that the one making the crossing is part of the tribe, and part of a story larger than their own. When the couple exchange wedding rings and recite their vows, they are partaking in an act of union that many have done before and that many will do again. When the grieving family lowers the casket into a heavily populated cemetery, their grief is given context by this ritual's reminder that death comes to all, that it is a part of life that has to be accepted because it can't *not* be. One of the cruelest things that can happen in a story is for a person to be excluded from these rites by which we make sense of our lives—and sometimes one of the most heroic (and risky) acts in a story is when one such character insists on their own inclusion or when another character insists on their behalf.

Exercise 26

Those elves fleeing the dragon: suppose now that they have a warrior caste. What is that caste called? What vows do its members swear? How does one *become* a warrior—not just the training, but the ritual by which they take up these duties? Decide these things.

Now think of a character who might be excluded from that rite of passage and therefore from that caste—but who will nonetheless hold the secret, the ability, or the opportunity that will permit the dragon's defeat. Consider:

- On what basis were they excluded?
- How do they respond?
- Who speaks up on their behalf?
- What risks do they incur in their attempts to be recognized as one of the warriors and granted the resources, weapons, and rights that position confers—resources they will need, perhaps, to battle the dragon? What does their pursuit of being a warrior cost them?

PRIVILEGE

In your imagined society, who has privilege and who does not? *Privilege* refers specifically to the ability to move about one's day while doing only minimal work to ensure one's safety and survival. Those without privilege in the imagined civilization engage in a series of adaptive behaviors that are intended to increase their odds of safety or survival. They live with more fear, but they also perceive more details about their world and how it works. This is because their vigilance is a requirement for their survival, whereas it is not so for the privileged. The privileged are often unaware of the existence of these adaptive behaviors.

In our own society, for example, men generally have the privilege of doing less work to survive than women do. Where a middle-class man may walk through a parking garage straight to his car, unlock the door, jump in, and drive away, a woman of the same class may handle the return to her car differently. She may take out her keys when she first enters the garage, gripping them in her hand to provide an improvised weapon should one be needed for her defense. She may check the shadows around her carefully as she hurries to her car. Where the man may have strolled, she may adopt an aggressive, rapid, confident walk meant to broadcast to any potential assailants that she is not an easy target and is not to be messed with. When she reaches her car, she may check the back seat prior to entering the vehicle, to ensure that no assailant has invaded the car during her absence and is now lying in wait. These are all adaptive behaviors that the man is less likely to engage in, and he may not even be aware that this woman who works in the same office has these adaptive behaviors. It may never have occurred to him that such behaviors might be necessary. The woman in this example, however, knows that she may be attacked if she is not vigilant; this is a very real possibility in her life. She may have been stalked or attacked in the past. She may know other women who have been. She may have been raised by her parents with persistent messages that she must be vigilant, on her guard, and ready to flee or defend her body from attack. Other forces in her society—stories and film, media and marketing, the voices of her peers, the vocal opinions of law enforcers or politicians—may also, and repeatedly, have affirmed to her that should she be attacked, others will judge her to have been at fault for not having been sufficiently vigilant, they will be unlikely to hold her assailant accountable for his actions. Thus, she has lists of habitual, adaptive behaviors that are intended to increase the odds of her survival, and that the man in our example has likely never felt the need to adopt. His lack of need for these behaviors and his lack of awareness that they exist is what we mean when we use the term *privilege*.

Other forms of privilege exist besides gendered privilege, of course. White parents in our culture can teach their children to dial 9-1-1 and call for a cop when in danger; parents of color do not always have the privilege of assuming that cops will defend and protect their children. Their fear when their children encounter law enforcers is an experience that may be alien to many who have more privilege in this society.

In Chapter 1, we discussed how defining the *physical* conditions for survival creates opportunities and imposes constraints on how your characters can navigate the physical spaces on their world, and what kinds of situations they will confront. Similarly, when you ask the question about your imagined civilization—"Who has privilege? Who doesn't?"—this can help you define the *social* conditions for survival and map out how your characters navigate the social spaces in their world. If your character is traveling from Point A to Point B, what must she do to protect herself on her journey? If your character is not a member of the privileged class, race, gender, sexual orientation, religion, or species, in what social spaces and what social groups will he feel safe or less safe? How will this affect how he acts, when he voices his opinion, what choices he makes during a sudden emergency?

Here are some questions to ask to help map this out:

- What injustices or perils pass largely without notice from the society's most comfortable group of people?
- What events do those characters permit through apathy or ignorance?
- What kind of experiences would wake those characters up?
- In the event of a crisis, whose voice is privileged? Whose voice is less likely to be believed, in this imagined culture?
- For those without privilege, what *adaptive behaviors* have they adopted in order to navigate this society and increase their odds of survival and safety?

If *you* are yourself a person with some privilege in our own society, it is worth taking the time to examine how this works—both as a citizen and as a storyteller. In your worldbuilding, understanding how privilege operates allows you to create imagined societies and situations that are more nuanced and subtle. For example, suppose your story involves ethnic or class or inter-species conflict within the space of, say, a single city or culture. Rather than depicting prejudice and the desire for equality in terms of chains, literal slavery, or laws that discriminate overtly, you might be able to write some incredible drama into your story simply by looking at *whose word gets believed* during a crisis. Who gets heard? Who gets dismissed as hysterical, hormonal, unreliable, or likely to be lying? In C.J. Cherryh's *Chanur saga,* for example, male hani are considered prone to bursts of testosterone that render them emotional, aggressive, and unreliable—so when a male has something to say, the female hani pat him gently on the paw and pretend to listen but don't really assign much weight to his words. They conceal entire areas of daily life from him, and they don't permit him to travel with them, believing that a male hani on a starship would be a highly emotional, unstable threat to ship and crew at worst and a burden on their efficiency at best.

A different example: in Suzanne Collins' *Catching Fire,* the second volume of *The Hunger Games*, there is a scene in which Katniss and Peeta attend a banquet at the Capitol. They witness the wealthy citizens of the Capitol gorging themselves on expensive delicacies and then vomiting into little glasses so that they can empty their bellies enough to experience still *more* delicacies. Because Katniss has spent much of her life hunting turkeys and rabbits in the wood to keep her starving family alive, this abundance and waste of food is shocking to her. Hearing what the citizens around her use the little glasses for makes her feel ill and enraged. The other citizens have the privilege of never having had to worry about whether their next meal will fail to arrive; Katniss and her District have not enjoyed that same privilege. All of this—and the emotional impact of it for the character—is illustrated to the reader with that tiny detail of the little vomit glasses. That's good, efficient worldbuilding…and good storytelling.

Conversely, suppose you are writing a more utopian society in which there is *less* prejudice, discrimination, and bigotry than there is in our own. In that case, understanding the mechanics of how privilege operates can help you imagine with more clarity how such a society might operate differently on a day-to-day basis, how people might act and talk and approach decisions differently. It can help you make that society more realistic.

For some of my readers, understanding privilege, surviving without much privilege, and navigating around those who have privilege is part of their daily lives. If this isn't you, however, or if the idea of "privilege" sounds uncomfortable, political, or irrelevant to you, some resources that can help you understand how privilege works include Ta Nehisi Coates' *Between the World and Me* or Ijeoma Oluo's essays on the subject (go to http://www.ijeomaoluo.com/about for links). If you are a male writer and you want a brief window into the perceptions and adaptive behaviors of the women in your life, I would recommend asking. You can also read the collection *Dear Men* at https://stantlitore.com/men-can-you-hear-us—but really, there are dozens of feminist bloggers who can provide eye-opening insight and whose work can easily be found with a little quick Googling. I encourage you to do this. It is worth doing because grasping the differences between how those with more safety and those with less safety perceive and navigate their daily lives greatly expands the storytelling opportunities available to you, increasing the depth and nuance you can write into your imagined world. It is also worth doing because it will help you better understand the non-fictional world in which you breathe and work and live each day.

Exercise 27

Come up with a love story between two (or more) elves. One of the elves involved has considerably more privilege than the other(s). Perhaps this elf has camouflage granted by the society's elders (because of his family connections or status) that permits safe night-passage through the carnivore-haunted swamp. Perhaps this elf desires a moonlit tryst with the intended lover(s) under the mangroves and cypresses. It might never occur to this elf that the lover(s) might be less safe. How does the scene play out? Does the other elf agree to the tryst? How much work and preparation does this other elf do to make themselves safer on the journey out to the place where the lovers will meet? Are they late? Are they exhausted? Does this occasion an argument? Perhaps the more privileged lover thinks the other, being late, is yearning less, or is less in love? Or perhaps the more privileged elf pushes for more affection than can be given when the other is exhausted from the terrors of the swamp? Or does the late-arriving lover say something that both hurts the privileged lover and shocks them with sudden awareness of how much they don't know about their lover's life and its challenges? What happens on this night? How do the events of this tryst shape the elves' relationship, either for better or for worse?

LAW, JUSTICE, AND CRIME

Let's go back to the idea of home. An especially useful question for the storyteller and worldbuilder is: Who is banished from home? Who is excluded from the community? Who has (and doesn't have) rights to appeal to the authorities to recover a place in the community? We have seen that the idea of home is bound up in the two questions *What are we sheltering from?* and *Who are we sheltering?* We have seen how the answers to these questions drive architecture, rites of passage, and the way people tell their history (the story of their home). Now let's look at how these questions drive the community's sense of law and order.

In other words, you might explore, through the eyes of this imagined culture: Who is seen as a threat? And who needs to be protected?

How does your imaginary society govern, legislate, and regulate its members? What acts are labeled criminal in this culture? Who responds to crime, and how effectively? What are the penalties for crime (fines? Forced labor? Imprisonment? Death?)? Who writes the laws, who interprets them, and who enforces them? And especially, what parties or factors have power to influence the writing, interpreting, and enforcement of the laws?

What ideals about justice does this imaginary culture hold most dear? For example, in our own culture, we have the ideal that "justice is blind," by which we mean *impartial.* This leads us to try our best effort at constructing a judicial system that will enact our desire that everyone be subject equally to the laws and to their enforcement, regardless of their status, their wealth, or their demographics, so that "no one is above the law." These are values we say that we hold and that we intend to live up to.

Of course, there is a wide gap between the values we *say* we hold and the values we *actually* hold—and that gap can create tension for an imagined world and for your story, just as it creates (unfortunately) real tension in our own world and in the real stories of people's lives in our world. For example, we know that our judicial system assigns penalties and protections disproportionately based on race. This is not an accident—it is because generations of people have desired that upstanding white citizens be protected from "thugs," "gangsters," and the "lawless," by which they meant people with darker skin tones. That fear of the other and that desire to exclude the other from walled, middle-class, "safe" neighborhoods—to shelter white homes against the imagined threat of the black other—has proven so strong for so long that it has been written invisibly but potently into our judicial system. It feeds implicit biases in how juries consider evidence, in the language prosecutors use, and in the severity of judges' sentencing. Similarly, in your imagined world, what unspoken prejudices determine whom the laws protect and whom the laws punish?

In approaching this issue as a storyteller, I have found Jacques Derrida's description of the gap between *law* and *justice* to be very useful. Here, *justice* is the name we give to an event that we are always waiting for. We are hoping justice will be served; we are hoping that the violence and cruelty in our society will be replaced with fairness and safety. *Justice* is the name we assign to an imagined ideal, a hoped-for future condition that is always just out of reach and that is ours to strive for. *Law* is the system by which we attempt to bring that event to pass.

The reason that a gap exists between the two is that *justice* is specific, while *law* is general. If the event of justice were to be fully realized, the needs of each individual in the community would be fairly met; by definition, justice is specific and particular. Law, however, is our best attempt at making justice real by identifying rules and solutions that apply generally to the greatest number of cases and serve the needs of the greatest number of individuals. But no matter how impartial we think the law is, someone's needs will be unaccounted for. Someone will always be left out. For this reason, there is always a gap between law and justice. Various factors—from cultural prejudices and fears, to corruption, to lack of due process—can widen that gap. Because that gap exists and because its existence costs lives, there are always voices in the culture who point out the gap, who speak truth to power and call upon their fellow citizens to close the gap. If the gap is narrow, these voices may urge reform. If the gap is wide, these voices may urge revolution.

What widens that gap in your imagined world? Who wants to narrow it? And who benefits from it staying exactly the way it is?

Try writing a few laws for your imagined society. While doing this, come up with answers to the following questions:

- Name two ideals that are enshrined in the legal system in your imagined civilization. What are they, and what are their implications for how "justice" gets served, and to whom? Examples: *Order; Peace; Respect for authority; Safety of the populace; Ownership of property; Pure moral conduct; Piety toward the gods.*

- What person or group is tasked with making the laws? What are their hopes, fears, and goals? What do they bring with them to this process?

- What person or group is tasked with interpreting and judicating the laws? What are their hopes, fears, and goals? What do they bring with them to this process?

- What person or group is tasked with enforcing the laws? What are their hopes, fears, prejudices, and goals? In what ways do they have the population under surveillance?

- Who is most protected by these laws and their enforcement? Who is sheltered by the law? Whose home is protected?

- Who suffers most under these laws and their enforcement? Who is seen as a threat to the home?

- Which of the groups above do your main characters belong to? How does this influence the way they go about their daily lives, and how does this influence how they perceive and interact with each other?

Here are two exercises that can help you translate these concepts into opportunities for vivid world-creation and thrilling storytelling:

Exercise 28

Imagine a society of sentient insect-creatures. Values include worship of the queen, hard work, and loyalty to the hive. The laws are written by the drones who mate with and serve the queen, and are enforced and judicated by warrior-insects who are genetically engineered for this purpose; these warriors are, as the saying goes, judge, jury, and executioner all in one. For this fictional society:

- Write at least three laws. Think about what is required of worker-insects in this society. What might constitute a crime?
- What might motivate a main character to break one of these laws (or several of them)?
- What would happen next? If they go fugitive, how does your main character elude the relentless mandibles of insect-justice?
- Who aids them in their flight?
- Who betrays them?
- Who pursues them?
- What are their options? (Are we working toward a thrilling climax in which they sneak into the heart of the hive to lay their appeal at the feet of the queen? Are they hoping to escape the hive altogether? Do they try to erase the memory of their crime?)

And, of course, reverse-engineer the world accordingly. Find the world that would make the most exciting version of this scenario possible:

- What are the physical conditions for survival in this hive or in the world outside it?
- What prodigious and perhaps predatory animals might try to attack your fugitive now that they cannot rely on the protection of the hive's warrior-enforcers?
- What are the various worse-case scenarios in this world, outcomes that your story could flirt with briefly before rescuing character and reader in the adrenaline rush of a well-timed action sequence?

Exercise 29

This time, imagine a society that lives within a hollowed asteroid. Population numbers and access to life-critical resources might be tightly controlled.

- What would an illicit (or illegal) love affair look like on this world? What would make it illegal? What would happen if the lovers were caught? Outline a few plot points accordingly.
- What does a black market look like on this asteroid? Come up with one good that is secretly available for sale.
- Briefly sketch out two characters who might seek to buy this good illegally but for very different reasons.
- Briefly sketch out the character who is complicit in allowing the black market to persist. What kind of "fee" does he exact from the underground world in return for his complicity and silence, and for what purpose does he exact this fee? Make it interesting, something other than simple greed. Maybe his daughter—or his mother, or his brother—suffers a debilitating and chronic illness, and there is a drug in

the black market that can at least relieve her pain, and this motivates him to confiscate doses from the druglords in return for allowing their operations to continue. What other motives could you imagine? What risks does this character undertake by doing this?

FIND THE ONE UNFORGETTABLE FACT

What we've looked at in this chapter are an array of strategies that can help you either identify your imagined culture's most significant difference...or identify intriguing details that will reveal that difference.

Keep returning to that one truly unforgettable fact about your fictional culture. Provide other details to the reader in ways that cast fresh light on this key difference and that help the reader to grasp the significance that particular cultural trait has for the characters. These may be details that confirm our first impression of this culture, or that complicate our impressions.

For the Fremen in *Dune*, that one unforgettable fact is the absolute need to conserve water, so Frank Herbert shares details that throw that fact into harsh relief. So we learn that the Fremen reclaim water from the dead; that spitting at the feet of a visiting Duke is a sign of respect, not an insult; that tears—"giving water to the dead"—are wondrous to the Fremen and that weeping is a sacred and rare act.

For the Dothraki in George R. R. Martin's *A Song of Ice and Fire*, one distinct fact of their culture is that everything of importance in life must be done under the open sky.

From that point, all the other details proceed: their life of marauding on horseback; their disdain for walls and roofs; outdoor weddings; and the fact that seduction is best achieved not by leading one's lover into a secluded and private tent but instead by leading your lover out into the grasses under the stars.

For the Vor in Lois McMaster Bujold's *Barrayar*, the key fact is the fear of mutation. This is emphasized to the reader by the infanticide in the rural mountain towns; by the absolute authority of the father over the Barrayan household, an authority rooted in the father's duty to safeguard the family's genes by accepting or rejecting infants; by the reactionary fear of anyone who looks different; by the way this fear is expressed in xenophobic warfare; by the abuse that a dwarf receives.

All right, let's get back to our elves fleeing their dragon. What is the most unforgettable fact of the elves' culture? The key trait that we might spend a novel exploring?

Suppose that unforgettable fact is the desire (and ability) to speak to flying creatures and influence those creatures to do their will. Imagine how we might add other details to show this to the reader:

- Elven babies, when born, are immediately wrapped in a cloak of feathers designed to look like wings.

- Elven elders, when dead, are buried in a shroud of feathers.

- Elven spouses enter the wedding ceremony naked, and dress each other in feathers. Once they are both winged, the ceremony is complete. "Fly together in love," the matriarch tells them. "Take care never to break your lover's wings. Take care never to put your lover in a cage."

- Elven children are taught to sing birds down from the sky, to perch on their hands.

- Elves may be prejudiced against those who cannot sing birds out of the sky, and these individuals have difficulty finding spouses. Perhaps they are even relegated to lives of service or slavery.

In our story, however, a dragon is not like a turtle-dove or a nightingale. A *dragon* cannot be sung out of the sky. Cannot be persuaded. Cannot be bent to an elf's will. Yet a dragon is a flying creature. What a horror and a shock this must be to the elves! Perhaps it as though they are all suddenly voiceless, all as "disabled" as those individuals they have previously scorned and enslaved. Will this cause upheaval in their society, adding additional urgency and tension to the story beyond just the struggle for survival? If one of the characters is a slave who has never been able to call a bird, will that character respond to the crisis differently? Whereas the other elves are lost in panic and dismay at the failure of what appears to be an essential elven ability, the elf that has always lived without that ability may be able to keep a more level head.

Or maybe we choose to explore some other fact that makes this elven culture unforgettable. Here is an exercise that will help:

Exercise 30

Choose one of the following three possible "unforgettable facts" about this elven culture.

Option A: Elves are vegetarian and have been for the past two centuries; no modern elf will take the life of an animal.

Option B: No elf will willingly stand exposed to the daylight sun.

Option C: Elves believe in being rooted to one place and resist long travel or the abandonment of a home; the oldest elves literally grow rooted into one place like a tree, their feet digging deep into the earth and their outer skin hardening.

Now, brainstorm five ways to explore that one cultural trait in greater detail. Specifically, decide how that one trait is expressed by: 1) the society's laws, 2) its rites of passage, 3) its monuments and relics, 4) their technology or magic, and 5) their religion(s) or their most important stories about who they are.

Finally, after unpacking how that trait is expressed in various details of their culture, answer this last question: **How does this fact about their culture *complicate* their struggle to survive a dragon? What options do the characters have for getting around those complications during their flight or fight with the dragon?**

THE PATRIARCHY DOESN'T HAVE TO WIN EVERY TIME

A final note. You're imagining a new world populated by a new culture that designs for itself a new kind of home. The fictional culture and home may have significant perils and flaws. But your world doesn't have to repeat all of *our* world's mistakes. Reverse some of those, or skip them entirely.

Be interesting—make new mistakes instead.

Consider the worlds of *Kushiel's Dart*, of *The Left Hand of Darkness*, of *The Pride of Chanur*, of *Binti*. Such examples show us that not every world has to be one where one gender dominates all others, where rape is commonplace, or where the very structure of the world lends itself easily to the story of one "strong female character" going it alone in a world of hostile men. We've all read that story. I've *written* that story, in the past—I'm as guilty as any of that failure of imagination.

But I want to write and read new stories and imagine new worlds. So I would encourage you to be brave in your imagining. What might an *entirely* different social structure look like? Our culture's particular concerns with gender and power are a product of basic premises that were shaped by our ancestors' responses to their environment long ago. You are writing a world with a different environment, different flora and fauna, and different cultural responses. Show us that world!

And if you're in search of a little social commentary, you don't have to replicate our culture's specific issues and dynamics in order to achieve that. You could replace or subvert—or at least invert—them. In her *Chanur* saga, C. J. Cherryh writes a society in which only women travel and hunt and fare through space; only women handle commerce; men are believed too hormonally unstable and are relegated to defend and secure the home, putting their testosterone to use at the doors of their estate. And same-gender romantic relationships between female mariners are not uncommon. Cherryh then tells the story of a merchant captain who smuggles her mate aboard ship and takes him to the stars, and all the issues that ensue from that. It's also a story about a lot of other things too—but that's one part of it, and it's very compelling and riveting to read and very topical in its understated but unmistakable social commentary. And it's also very human, despite the fact that the characters involved are mostly cat aliens.

If we can imagine a world where people ride on the backs of giant sandworms across endless desert or a world where a teenager can walk into the waters of death and ring magical bells to silence the ravenous dead, we can certainly imagine a world where the premises and hang-ups of the cultures we encounter on the page are different ones from our own. Show us worlds we haven't seen before, so that when we close the book we can return to our own with fresh vitality and clarity (and even hope). Or at least so that all of your readers—of varied ethnicities, genders, and sexual orientations—can have a really fun time while they sojourn in your book. Go and do that.

5. SHARING YOUR STRANGE NEW WORLD WITH THE READER

IT'S NOT QUITE ENOUGH simply to write a beautiful world, populated by beautiful characters living out beautiful stories. You also have to invite a reader into that world, which is easier said than done. After all, you're asking a reader to spend a part of their life in your story, exploring these wonders or horrors hatched from your imagination. How do you excite them about your fictional world—and how do you guide them through it without handing them a 'bible' or encyclopedia or dungeon guide documenting all the details and rules of the world they're entering?

That's what we'll look at in this chapter. We'll talk about two strategies in particular: defining a threshold for the reader to cross, and providing them with a local guide. There is a third thing you need—and if you read the companion book *Write Characters Your Readers Won't Forget*, you'll find an entire book that unpacks that third thing, which is a character readers fall in love with, who is living a story they want to experience. We'll talk about that here a little, as well, because *world* and *character* are interdependent on each other—but most of what we'll review in this chapter has to do specifically with guiding the reader through the world.

And to do that, you will want to identify your threshold text and the reader's in-world guide. So let's talk about those. Then, at the end of the chapter, we'll take a look at strategies for sharing detail about the imaginary world in the right amount at the right times. We will look both at how to "show, don't tell" and how to "tell, don't show."

That's what is ahead. Here we go!

THE THRESHOLD TEXT

As one of my editors is fond of asking me, "What is your threshold text?" The importance of this crossing of the threshold has been noted by Maureen Quilligan in *The Language of Allegory*, Joseph Campbell in *The Hero with a Thousand Faces*, and Andrew Hallam in "Thresholds to Middle-Earth." It's a powerful concept for a storyteller. Let's take a look.

In Chapter 1, I used the metaphor of a house to describe the world of the story. Now imagine that in opening your book to the first chapter, your reader is at the doorstep of your story. Like a vampire, your reader needs to be invited in. The mechanism by which you invite them into the story is called a *threshold text*. Not only is this text an invitation to cross the threshold and begin the story, it also provides the reader with important cues about what *kind* of story this is, what kind of world they are entering, and how they should approach entering it. Are they crossing into a military scene or a civilian one? An adventure or a more domestic scene?

The threshold is both *invitation* and *context*. The invitation excites the reader, either intriguing the mind or getting the blood pumping. Simultaneously, the context relaxes the reader, by providing just enough information for them to get "lost" in the story.

If you were teleported in the very next minute from your comfortable chair to a strange forest world, that might be both exciting—and scary or unsettling. Especially if a warband of Orcs charges out of the trees at you! But, if you are also provided by the invisible author with a classy set of armor, a sword or battle-axe, and a magical necklace that turns arrows away from their target (rather a handy device, if the target is *you*), then suddenly you have clues as to what kind of world and what kind of story you've landed in. A World of Warcraft raid, apparently. You know what role you've landed in, and what some of the options are. You can then either flee—or engage and go on reading the story.

In *Star Trek*, the Captain's Log at the beginning of each episode is a threshold text. The log centers the viewer in a story of exploration in space. You know that there's a mission. You know that this is a naval culture, with regulations and hierarchy. You're told, as the viewer, to follow the Captain. With that expectation set, our eyes are on Kirk. Of course, those expectations can be upended later. This might actually be Spock's story, or McCoy's, or Uhura's, or Sulu's. But the log entry provides a threshold through which you can step from your living room onto the bridge of the *U.S.S. Enterprise*.

Often the threshold text involves an *actual* threshold: a literal door in the character's world, like the door of a wardrobe into Narnia, or the door into a bookshop in *The Neverending Story*, or the door of the TARDIS, so much bigger on the inside. The reader crosses the threshold *with* the character.

For example, as Tolkien scholar Andrew Hallam argues, the threshold text into Middle-Earth is the door at Bag End. The story of *The Hobbit* opens with a stranger coming to the door—Gandalf, arriving unexpectedly to invite Bilbo the hobbit to go on an adventure. For Bilbo, that round green door of his house in the hill is a doorway to comfort. He routinely steps inside and relaxes into a comfortable, upper middle-class life. When he refuses the adventure, Gandalf marks a rune on the outside of his door. This both tells the traveling dwarves where to find Bilbo so they can whisk him away on adventure—and it changes the meaning of the door. By scratching the rune into the wood, Gandalf changes the door from a doorway into comfort to a doorway outward to adventure. In a few more scenes, Bilbo will in fact go running out that door in such a hurry to adventure that he will leave behind his hat and his handkerchief. And the reader will go running out with him.

In *Three Parts Dead*, the first novel in Max Gladstone's thrilling Craft Sequence, the threshold is also a literal door—though a very different one. At the beginning of the story, the mage Tara Abernathy, just graduated, is booted from her academy world and literally tossed out of a door in the sky. She plummets toward the earth, using her magic to slow her descent. That door in the sky and the reader's precipitous fall with Tara through a thousand feet of empty air provides both the invitation into this story and the context the reader needs at the outset to know what kind of story it is. It's a story that has magic and magic users in it, with Craft powerful enough to slow and survive a thousand-foot fall. And we also get hints that it's going to be a story about finding home and a vocation. Tara has a business card in her pocket from a more senior witch who wants to employ her. She has been exiled from her academy. Picking herself up in the Badlands, she trudges homeward to a rustic town where she no longer fits in. No more college—where will she live (with her parents? In a big city?)? How will she use her newfound talents? Where will she fit in and where will she work? That's the kind of story we're starting out in. We learn this very quickly (as one has to, when falling through the atmosphere), and then we're off.

In Garth Nix's *Sabriel*, the door is the First Gate between life and death. The story opens with the necromancer's daughter attempting to resurrect a friend's pet rabbit. She steps into the river of death and approaches the First Gate. Again, a threshold text. We could list many other examples. Gene Wolfe's *The Book of the New Sun* opens with Severian confronting a locked gate that becomes a symbol of his exile; Madeleine L'Engle's *A Wrinkle in Time* opens with a stranger's knock at the door of Meg's house in the middle of a storm; Ursula K. LeGuin's *The Left Hand of Darkness* begins with the envoy Genly Ai observing the construction of a gate; the action of *Star Wars* opens with a fleeing spaceship being drawn into the hangar bay door of a much larger vessel, followed by a door on the captured ship being blown open to let in Darth Vader and a flood of stormtroopers.

Less literal boundaries provide thresholds too. Peter S. Beagle's *The Last Unicorn* opens when two hunters cross the boundary into the unicorn's forest and deliver to her some unexpected and unwelcome news. In the first example we looked at—*Star Trek*—the Captain's Log is the threshold into a new day, a new Stardate on which new things will be discovered.

When writing your threshold text, these are six critical questions to ask:

1. What clues do I want to give the reader about the genre and the world of the story?

2. What rune will I scratch into this door? In other words, what makes this specific threshold significant? What clues should this threshold give the reader about the thematic concerns of my story?

3. What, literally, is the door or boundary into the story?

4. Do I ease them in (like Bilbo Baggins being wooed by a dinner party and dwarven music while he resists the pull of the Road outside his door) or do I shove them unceremoniously over the threshold (like Tara plummeting out of the sky)? Which approach best serves my story?

5. For my character, what are the risks of crossing this threshold?

6. Why must they cross it? What is to be gained?

These last two questions (#5 and #6) are important because the crossing of the threshold sets up or hints at the central conflict of the story, and because the character, in crossing that threshold, takes the reader with them. These questions require thinking about both the plot (What is the conflict?) and the story's thematic concerns (What does that conflict mean? How can we understand its significance?) Maureen Quilligan describes this as the purpose of the threshold text: to introduce and define the themes that will be at stake in the story.

The threshold includes a message for the reader, a message marked on that door for us to read, just like the rune that Gandalf scratches into Bilbo's door. In *Star Wars*, we know at once that we are in a story about conflict and underdog heroism; in *The Left Hand of Darkness*, a story of an outsider seeking entry into a culture he barely understands. In *A Wrinkle in Time*, the message is that the universe is much larger and more significant than either Meg Murray or the reader expects. There are storms that might tear a house—or a person—apart. And coming in with the storm, there is Mrs. Whatsit, observing that "by the way, there *is* such a thing as a tesseract."

Andrew Hallam adds that crossing this threshold is just the beginning, suggesting themes that the rest of the story will require both character and reader to interpret. What happens when the character crosses the threshold, takes the risk, and begins the story? Besides initiating a plot, the conflict in that moment raises questions in the reader's head and heart—questions that can only be answered by finishing the story. *Can* a band of underdog heroes elude and overcome an evil empire, if their cause is just and they have the grit to see it through? What will the costs of rebellion be? Does love conquer all? Is blood thicker than water? What truly makes a person beautiful? Why do human beings tend toward violence? How do we seek justice in an unjust society? You get the idea—whatever thematic questions are at stake in your novel or story, the threshold text is what invites the character and the reader to wrestle with them.

In my novel *What Our Eyes Have Witnessed*, that first threshold is the door of Caius Lucius Justus's office on the Palatine Hill in Rome. He is the urban praetor, charged with overseeing justice in the city, and this story opens when one of the unquiet and ravenous dead bursts through his office door, disrupting everything he believes about the stability and order in his city. The event also challenges his belief in the unshakable superiority of the patrician class, because this zombie is not the corpse of a day-laborer or brothel-keeper—the kinds of people Caius tends to blame all the city's problems on—but a senator's daughter; Caius recognizes the family ring she wears. Not only has a physical and social threshold been crossed; it has been shattered and transgressed. The story opens with a violated threshold, introducing a novel that is all about violated boundaries (one of which is the boundary between life and death).

Now, this novel doesn't begin with the actual breaking of the door but with the scene five minutes later—with Caius crouching by the (now inert) body beside that threshold. Caius notes the corpse's patrician dress, its wounds, its festering stench, the ring on the hand, putting together the clues like a detective to find out who this corpse had been and what kind of larger threat to the offices and traditions of Rome might be signified by the broken door into his office.

This choice of where to open the scene and how to present the violated threshold signals to the reader that rather than just a story of zombie-fighting action, the reader is entering into a bit of detective-work. (In fact, the scenes ahead will lead to a courtroom drama, even if the court case *is* interrupted by the rampaging dead). The game is afoot, and it is a game of interpretation. What does the presence of the zombies mean? What is causing this threat? How will the threat be met? Who is equipped to meet it? In the next moment, after Caius has had the inert zombie dragged from his office, another character, Polycarp, is brought in, and a duel of wills and a battle of interpretations begins between two distinguished old men who have very different notions of what causes a zombie epidemic in the streets of Rome and what's to be done in response to it.

Find your threshold text, and not only do you find the way to invite your reader into the specific kind of adventure you're having—you also discover things that will clarify to you, the author, what your story is *most* about.

Exercise 31

Select three of your favorite fantasy or science fiction movies or novels—ones not mentioned yet in this chapter. You may need to rewatch the first ten minutes or reread the first chapter. See if you can identify:

- What is the threshold or boundary the reader is invited to cross?
- What hints are given to the reader about what kind of world this is?
- What hints are given to the reader about the thematic concerns of the story?
- Were you eased over the door into the house—carried in gently like a bride, perhaps—or were you thrown through the door?

Now, once you have these questions answered, engage in a thought experiment. Imagine changing some of the answers. What if the first threshold crossed was some *other* door in the story? Imagine if the story had opened *that* way instead. How would a different threshold have made your experience of that story different?

For example, how would *Star Trek* look different if it opened not with the Captain's Log, but with an alien on one of the planets visited stepping out their door into the street and looking up to see a giant starship suddenly hanging in their sky? Whose story would it be? What might some of the perspectives and concerns of that story be? What if *The Lion, the Witch, and the Wardrobe* began not with a wardrobe inside a mansion but with the gate to the courtyard of statues at the White Witch's House? Perhaps one of the children is hiding from Wolves and is running through the courtyard *to* the gate, trying to escape before they can be eaten or turned into stone. What kind of story would open in that way, and how would it feel different from the one we know?

Use this thought experiment to examine how threshold texts work, how they deliver clues to the reader, and how you can use them. Take note of how important and meaningful the specific thresholds you've crossed to get into your favorite stories are! If you have a manuscript you are working on currently, play with the idea of identifying different thresholds the reader might cross in that first chapter. How many different options do you have for inviting the reader into the story—how many different doors?—and which of those options invites your reader inside in the most exciting way *and* in the way that best equips them for the story ahead?

THE IN-WORLD GUIDE

Once you have a threshold that signals to the reader what kind of story this is, the reader needs a character to invite them over that threshold. So the question is: Who invites the reader-vampire inside? And how does that character continue to guide the reader through the house that is your story?

Like Dante Alighieri visiting the *Inferno* or flying through *Paradiso*, your reader will likely have at least one Virgil or Beatrice to guide them through your imagined world. At least one. There may be multiple guides, and they may vary in their reliability. These are your main viewpoint characters, and there are a number of perspectives you can select from; each will guide your reader into the world differently. If you read *Write*

133

Characters Your Readers Won't Forget, you will learn some strategies for mapping your character's journey through the novel, but another way to think about character is to focus on your *reader*'s journey through the novel. What kind of guide are you providing to your reader? Let's look at a few options.

The Innocent

Taran Assistant Pig-Keeper. Frodo Baggins. Luke Skywalker. In this case, you have a character to whom the world outside their home is largely unknown. Because the world is almost as unknown to the main character as it is to the reader, as the writer you get to dramatize the discovery of the world and allow the reader to experience wonder vicariously. So when Frodo goes to Rivendell, it is *his* first time going there. Frodo and the reader experience the wonder of that place together.

A variation on the "innocent" is the "surveyor"—a more informed and scientific guide but one who is nonetheless also encountering the strange world for the first time, just as the reader is doing. Examples include the biologist venturing into Area X in Jeff Vandermeer's *Annihilation*, the Doctor in many *Doctor Who* plotlines, and the ship captains of *Star Trek* and various "explorer" SF sub-genres.

The innocent/surveyor guide is a typical choice for journey narratives and quest narratives. You often start at the character's home (or ship, or base camp), grounding both the reader and character in an experience of home before sending them out the door and onto the road.

The advantage of this perspective is that it is easy to invite the reader into the experience of wonder, and it is also easy to drop a lot of information in the reader's hands without disrupting the story, because you have a character who needs and seeks that information. Information about the world is as precious to the character as it is to the reader.

The disadvantage of this perspective is that it is tremendously over-used. You can only write Luke Skywalker so many times. So if you select this guide, your reader will be best served (and most entertained) if you find some new way to deploy this guide.

Jeff Vandermeer achieves this in *Annihilation* by offering us an unreliable narrator who conceals things about herself and her world from the reader, and by crafting a story where the drama is not only created by the character's encounter with the strange world but by the gap between what the character perceives and what is actually there, and by the literal ways in which that world transforms the character and makes her strange—to herself, to other characters, and to the reader. Of course, most quest narratives and exploration stories involve the transformation of the character, but usually this involves a shift in beliefs and values or a transformation of various moral or ethical traits and behaviors. In *Annihilation*, the transformation is rather more thorough and riveting.

The Invader

A further variation is the "invader" perspective: one who is discovering the world while attempting to subjugate or destroy it. Such a perspective often lends itself well to a tale told by the villain, or to a "change of heart" or "gone native" story. *Dances with Wolves* and its many imitations are stories of this kind. Such stories are difficult to do well; they frequently fall into familiar patterns and tropes, of which one of the most common is the trope of the "white savior." That is a main character who switches sides and saves the "natives" who (in the story) can't save themselves without this savior's intervention. It is lazy worldbuilding that is unlikely to be appreciated by readers who identify with the "natives" more than with the "white savior" in the story.

For an example of an "invader" perspective done well (and without falling back on the "white savior" trope), read Joseph Brassey's *Skyfarer*, in which a Vader-like villain provides one of the novel's two viewpoint perspectives that grant readers access to the imaginary world. (The other of the two is a surveyor/explorer perspective.) This villain's story and perspective is more fascinating than most because the villain is clearly an unreliable narrator, and his journey involves waking up to how thoroughly he has been brainwashed. His switching of sides is handled not as a savior action but as an atonement.

The Embedded Perspective

The opposite approach to the "innocent" is the "embedded" character. In this case, you share the imaginary world with the reader by dropping them right into the perspective and the life of a character who grew up in that world, a character to whom that world is not alien at all. This makes more demands on both reader and writer (because you don't have the device of the character learning the world, you have to convey a lot to the reader through actions, behaviors, and details that this character may take for granted), but the rewards of this approach are also significant. Like foreign language immersion, the reader has to get acquainted with the world quickly but then feels they have more of a place in it. They, like the character, are grounded in the experience. You then create suspense, tension, and story not by flinging the innocent character into worlds they don't know but by bringing unexpected or invading elements into the world they do know. C. J. Cherryh is a master at this; her *Chanur* saga tells the story of first contact between humanity and other species not through the eyes of the human explorer but through the embedded perspectives of the non-human merchants who rescue the explorer. We get immersed in their spacefaring world quickly; the strange and unexpected element that shakes up their world and provides the momentum in the plot is the human explorer (who is *not* the point-of-view character) and his pursuers, who will stop at nothing to reacquire him. We are fascinated by the human "Tully," but we experience that fascination through the curiosity of the hani merchanters. With the hani, we experience the anxiety of losing one's cargo, of making difficult hyperspace jumps, of issuing reports to the homeworld that are unlikely to be well-received, and of coping with the presence of a stowaway on what *was* a smoothly-functioning ship with a routine schedule. No longer. Now we're dumped into this story of chase and pursuit, seen through the eyes of Pyanfar and her increasingly weary—but brave—crew.

The Immigrant

Genly Ai in *The Left Hand of Darkness*. Cordelia Naismith in *Shards of Honor* and *Barrayar*. This approach combines some of the strengths of both the "innocent" and the "embedded" perspectives. Here you have a character who is learning the culture from an outsider's perspective, like the reader, but rather than journeying from culture to culture, they are engaged in the attempt to embed themselves into the new culture. They are trying to grow roots there—and much of the drama of the story can come from the conflicts and obstacles they encounter in that attempt. The advantage of this perspective is that you can explore your world deeply by contrasting it directly with another. Your character can comment directly on the differences. We learn much of what we know about Barrayar, for example, through Cordelia's pointed commentary and her struggles as she marries into and tries to adapt to a culture that is hostile to much of what she believes and values.

A variation on this perspective is to write from the viewpoint of the character who returns home after having been away. The character has been changed by the events of their absence; returning home, they find that home looks very different to them. The reader learns about the world through those differences. A wonderful example of this is Tara Abernathy in the first chapter of Max

Gladstone's *Three Parts Dead*; after years at a school for mages, Tara returns to the small country town she grew up in, where she must conceal much of her Craft and where she attempts and fails to fit back in.

The Disinherited

Here are two reasons that we enjoy stories of the disinherited—meaning those who are marginalized, oppressed, or unhomed in these imagined societies. First, the magnitude of the conflict and the height of the obstacles that must be climbed over is greater. A character who is without a home, who has more to *fear* from cops than to *hope* from them, or who lacks many of the privileges and rights the society grants to others, has the odds stacked against them—and we enjoy stories about overcoming the odds. The greater the odds, the greater the victory. Second, these perspectives allow us the deepest exploration into an imagined world. Remember the section on *privilege* in the previous chapter? Those with privilege often perceive less of what is happening in their world than do those who lack privilege, because the privileged don't need to be as vigilant in order to ensure their survival and safety; the actions required of them to ensure safety are minimal. As readers, though, even if we are readers who experience privilege in our own worlds, we crave to perceive *much*. Characters who lack privilege see more of their world and can show the reader more of how that world actually works. For example, consider how *Bladerunner* would be a very different film if it was told entirely through the privileged point of view of the CEO of Tyrell Corporation rather than through the disinherited eyes of that corporation's products and victims.

Exercise 32

Let's return to our tale of elves fleeing a dragon. I want you to outline (or write) a chapter in which the elves are attacked by the dragon. This will be the reader's first encounter with both elves and dragon. Write three versions of this scene, from three different perspectives, three different guides that each lead the reader through the chapter in their unique ways. Each guide will notice different details. And the scene in all of its horror and all of its adrenaline will have a different emotional impact for each of these three guides.

- First, write the scene from Alua's perspective. Alua is the greatest archer in the clan, she is middle-aged, and she is the sister of the matriarch. She has an *embedded* perspective.

- Second, tell the story from Rokko's perspective. Rokko married into the clan a month ago, but he comes from another clan far across the swamp, one with different customs and perspectives on the world. Rokko has an *immigrant* perspective.

- Third, tell the story from Sanaia's perspective. As a young slave, Sanaia has a *disinherited* perspective.

If you find the three scenes still sounding too alike, we can take a cue from my other course, *Write Characters Your*

Readers Won't Forget: Identify what is most at stake for each character in the scene.

For example, perhaps what is at stake for Alua is that she has been hiding from her clan the fact that her vision is failing and she is no longer able to shoot her arrows with accuracy; she wishes to both protect her clan from the dragon *and* continue hiding the changes in her body and ability.

Perhaps Rokko wants to be accepted by the clan and is trying to be a hero in ways that actually endanger the clan and his spouse.

Perhaps Sanaia wants to get free—or wants one of the masters to die (perhaps Alua, or perhaps Rokko's spouse.)

So each of these characters has obstacles to face and something that they want out of the scene. That gives each of them the ingredients for a conflict that you can write. Now consider: How does the world, the dragon, and the events that occur in this scene look different to each character? How, in each case, do you introduce the reader to the elven civilization and culture? What gets highlighted or foregrounded in each version? What do you judge most important to let the reader know? What does your reader *have* to know in order to understand the world and what is happening in it, as well as grasp what matters to the character who is the 'guide' for that scene?

HOW TO "SHOW, DON'T TELL": BEYOND THE INFO-DUMP

So you have your first threshold, and you have a local guide. Now how do you manage that guiding? Let's return to one of the questions we addressed in Chapter 1: How much detail about the world do you need? When we first looked at this question, it was from the perspective of how much detail the storyteller needs to *know* in order to tell the story. But there's a parallel question, which is how much detail the storyteller needs to *reveal* to the reader. Exercise 32, above, is a good example of how I would urge you to find answers to this question.

The answer to how much detail to share is simply this:

> Prior to each critical scene, what does my reader need to know, feel, or experience—in order for that scene to be clear and powerful?

In answering that question, create a short list of details. Then find the most efficient, dramatic, and entertaining way to share those details. Maybe through dialogue. Maybe through action. Here are a few examples.

Example A: Sanaia

Referring back to Exercise 32 above, let's take the example of Sanaia. If you are writing Sanaia's scene, your reader needs quick details that illustrate a few pieces of information: what Sanaia's duties have been, how Sanaia feels about those duties, what 'slavery' means in this culture, and what restrictions exist on Sanaia's movements or actions. You can reveal a lot of this, by the way, through action. Maybe the scene opens with the dragon attack and with the choice Sanaia makes in that moment to violate the restrictions on her activity. By letting the reader in on what that violation of the rules entails and how deeply Sanaia feels the risk, you may be able to reveal much about this culture's slavery and its attitudes, without having to dump lots of unnecessary detail. In other words, pick just the details that are relevant. You can reveal your worldbuilding through sensory detail: the thumping of Sanaia's heart and the quickening of fear at the sight of a whip on another's belt may paint half the picture that we need of Sanaia's position in this world.

Similarly, you can reveal some of whether we're in a cold or a hot landscape with a few details about clothing, wind, sweat, etc.

Example B: Alua

Or maybe you are writing Alua's scene. Maybe the scene opens with warning shouts and the bursting of a nearby tree into flames. Maybe you reveal critical details about Alua's position within her culture—her warrior-craft and her status—by sketching out the quick list of what items she grabs before darting from her tent to face the dragon. What armor does she put on, in the few moments she has to do so? That bow she snatches up, what wood or animal is it carved from? Maybe this a quick adjective—the "whalebone bow"—or maybe it is a couple sentences of mini-story, sketching out how at age fifteen, to prove herself, she tracked a marshwhale nine days through the swamp, and how she was nearly crushed beneath it but she cut her way through its carcass and bore its ribs on her back to the village, to the cheers of her people. For decades she has been their greatest warrior, and now she faces her greatest task. There's some good worldbuilding detail revealed in that, though it needs only a few sentences on the page.

Maybe the challenge Alua faces now is a failure of depth perception. Her eyesight blurs and she misses her grab for the bow, and the surge of anger—or fear—as she makes the second grab and catches up her weapon paints a quick picture of what will be at stake for her in the scene that follows. She has a heroic reputation and a personal past to live up to. There are expectations riding on her. But where once she tracked the marsh-whale with keen eyes, now she can hardly see to grab her bow. (By the way, I hope she makes her shot and injures the dragon against all odds. I really want Alua to make that shot. But if this were your story, you would take it wherever you want it to go. Maybe she misses, and elves die as a consequence, and then in the next scene you could show their funeral customs briefly and thus reveal even more of their world in the course of telling your story.)

Example C: Rokko

Maybe you are revealing details through dialogue. Referring back to Exercise 32 again, maybe Rokko's scene begins in his spouse's arms, in tender but worried words following sex. Maybe his spouse is attempting to reassure him that the clan will accept him.

"But after I insulted Alua last night, I was sure she was going to put an arrow in my eye," he says.

His spouse answers, "Alua doesn't trust easily, but it's only that she cares for her people—"

"She doesn't care for me," he interrupts, and immediately regrets the words because he senses that his spouse, lying in his arms, is disappointed with his gloominess. He feels the distance opening between them even though their bodies are pressed together, and it scares him. If he loses her warmth, he has lost everything, truly everything. Then a dragon's scream rends the air, shocking them both, and the action of the scene begins.

Now, in a few quick lines of dialogue, you have revealed some essential details about the culture, details that will be important *for this specific scene*. We know that:

- Rokko is an outsider.
- There are archers, and Alua is presumably a good one.
- In this scene Rokko wants to prove himself to a people who do not trust him.

You might also have introduced select details about the physical environment in which Rokko and his spouse's lovemaking took place. Are they reclining on cushions? Cushions made of what? Is it a tent? A house? A treetop? How many other homes are clustered around them? How private is the space they're in? Does the spouse (what is her/his/their name, by the way?) joke that the whole village heard them taking joy in each other's bodies? Does this make Rokko feel proud—or embarrassed? Does his origin culture consider sex to be a private matter, or an act to be applauded publicly and shouted to the heavens?

You might have revealed, again with just a sentence, some taboos and some details about their relationship and the vulnerabilities involved. Maybe, in a sentence about the night they just enjoyed together, you revealed that Rokko's people do not make love with the woman on top, but Rokko's spouse rode him last night and he found nothing to complain about in the experience. Perhaps you use this detail to stress the distance—not only in geography but in custom—that is opening between Rokko and his people, and the simultaneous excitement and vulnerability Rokko feels at being an immigrant member of a foreign clan.

3 Things to Define

Let's recap. So how much detail do you offer in this first scene? You give the essential details that help the reader feel and understand the following:

1. What is *at stake* for the characters (that is, what do they each want during this scene?).
2. The *obstacles* in their way and the *risks* inherent in the choices they'll make in dealing with those obstacles.
3. The actual *logistics* of what is about to happen in the scene.

In fact, you can make one or two details reveal a lot of information at once; one opportunity can serve multiple purposes. As we saw above, finding out whether Rokko's sex with his spouse was private or not, and how the two of them feel about that, can be used to simultaneously show how many people are in the clan, the kind of houses they use, how close those homes are to each other and how tightly clustered, their attitudes toward sex, and, incidentally, how many people are nearby and therefore at risk of being a dragon's breakfast in another page or two.

HOW TO "TELL, DON'T SHOW": DOING AN ELEGANT INFO-DUMP

"Show, don't tell" is often good advice for an emerging writer, but it does privilege a specific kind of storytelling. "Telling" can be powerfully effective if you do it in an entertaining way. Consider the opening chapter of Susanna Clarke's *Jonathan Strange & Mr. Norrell*, which "dumps" information about both England's romantic history of magic and its somewhat stuffy and academic approach to magic in the story's present. Clarke relays the information briefly, wittily, and in a way that demonstrates the very society that is about to be shaken up by her character's arrival. The wry, witty prose that relates the specific and academic details of magic *fits* the drily academic characters who—along with the reader—will be shocked in a few pages when Mr. Norrell, claiming to be an actual practical magician, awakens all the stones of York Minster cathedral and sets them talking. Clarke's approach is effective— more than that, the way she relays detail about her world is *strategic*. The reason people who teach fiction often advise "show, don't tell," is because "tell" is our default, and relying unthinkingly on a default is dangerous for a storyteller. When we are operating unconsciously from our default set of tools and tactics, it is more likely that our writing will be lazy and our storytelling will be dull. But Clarke isn't "telling" by default. She is telling details intentionally to achieve specific dramatic effects. What she is doing is purposeful.

We might easily identify other such examples of "telling" that are intentional, purposeful, and entertaining. For example, Michael Crichton's *Jurassic Park* intersperses high-adrenaline dinosaur action with brief lectures on science or mathematics (usually delivered by one of the characters). This is effective because many of these characters are scientists and mathematicians, and so the sudden lecture feels appropriate to the characters; and because the story rests on the premise that there is a lot of scientific knowledge that hasn't reached the general public yet but that may be entertaining, exciting, or dangerous if it did; and because the action of the story hinges on how much scientific and technological knowledge the characters have. Characters who miss critical details end up mauled and eaten. Characters who understand essentials of biology, chaos theory, or computers are able to gather clues, solve mysteries, and stay alive. Knowledge is both currency and weapon in *Jurassic Park*: it is how we survive. The humble, always-ready-to-learn-more attitude of Ellie, Grant, and Ian Malcolm is contrasted with both the ambivalence of Mr. Hammond, who doesn't really care to know anything more than what he needs to make money, and whose ignorance leads to the creation of a park where poisonous plants occupy the public atrium simply because they look pretty, and the arrogance of Dr. Yu, who believes his current knowledge of the dinosaurs' genetics to be absolute and infallible. Neither Dr. Yu nor Mr. Hammond make it out of the book alive.

Crichton's frequent dropping of miniature essays into the novel serves as both a pacing tactic and a thematic strategy: *Jurassic Park* is, among other things, a parable about the importance of learning and of thinking through the choices we have to make. So Crichton expects his readers to learn as they go, and communicates as much to them. Learning about paleontology, genetics, and math is their price of admission for enjoying a story that in turn is all about how learning is our price of admission for enjoying our survival.

So when do you "tell" instead of "show"? When do you dump information on the page?

When there's a reason to.

A reason other than just "The reader needs to know this."

A reason that is central to how you're telling the story and what kind of story it is.

Exercise 33

Let's info-dump…effectively. Back to the elves and the dragon. This time, you aren't writing Sanaia's, or Alua's, or Rokko's scene, but Ptara's. Ptara is the grand-daughter of the matriarch, the one who is trying to make up for lost time by memorizing and recalling all her grandmother's stories and wisdom about the swamps, now when it is most needed. In the past, Ptara has slacked off; now there is a special urgency and remorse to her need to get this knowledge, and to get as much of it as possible. Maybe her grandmother is dying, and the grandmother's info-dumps, delivered in the form of stories or lessons, are always interrupted halfway through as she loses consciousness again, leaving both Ptara and the reader in suspense, frustrated, needing to know more. It is a race against time. Ptara (and the reader) need to know how to survive in the swamp. They need to know about the different kinds of dragons and their abilities. They need to know how to cast specific spells, what kinds of herbs there are and how they can be found. Et cetera.

Here is your assignment. Write a scene in which the grandmother-matriarch dumps information on Ptara and the reader, as she lies in her deathbed:

1. First, write out the entire info-dump.
2. Now, revise. Pick the moment where the grandmother loses consciousness and the info-dump ceases.

To help you in selecting that moment, consider:

- What is the earliest possible moment where the lesson can end and the reader will still have received critical information needed for the scenes that will follow?
- What is the moment where ending the lesson would be *most* frustrating for Ptara?

Finally, play with different ways to add tension to the scene. Are there moments in the middle where the grandmother's voice is too low to be heard, and Ptara misses critical details? Is there "telling" offered that is obscure to Ptara? Is it also obscure to the reader? When will the meaning of these details be revealed? What would be the *most* exciting way for Ptara to learn that meaning, later in the story?

For an example of a scene that operates in a similar way, see Yoda's death scene in *Return of the Jedi*. Information has to be relayed quickly, but Luke Skywalker may not be ready for it, and Yoda has a limited time to relay it before breathing his last. Yoda's final remark—"there is another Skywalker"—is really important information that remains (for a brief time) cryptic to both Luke and the audience.

So "telling" instead of "showing" is not bad in some absolute sense. Sometimes, it is a strategic choice.

CONCLUSION

What I hope this book has conveyed is the fun of finding the right strategy for worldbuilding and world-revealing in your story. And I hope I have offered examples of such strategies, enough to fire up your imagination and send you reaching for pen and paper (or for your laptop, or for your voice recorder).

It is nearly time to end this book, though as the Bard says, "parting is such sweet sorrow." And it is, because there is so much more—so very much more—we *could* talk about. We could talk about maps and whether they are two-dimensional or three-dimensional or four-dimensional, whether north is at the top or whether the holy city is at the center, who makes the maps and why, whose tools they are and whose they aren't. We could talk about disease and the role it plays in shaping and reshaping entire civilizations and ecosystems. We could talk about military tactics or what kind of species breathe methane instead of oxygen, or what the poets might sing in your imaginary world if there were fifty moons in the sky instead of one.

But all of that can be looked up.

All of that can be imagined.

My task here has been to show you some of what you can do, and provide a framework to help you navigate and focus the research, the imaginative play, and the writing up of details—so that each foray into the design of your world doesn't become overwhelming but remains exciting, a sequence of surprising discoveries and unexpected opportunities.

As you have seen, the framework is really simple: Find unforgettable physical conditions for survival. Find an unforgettable creature (at least one). Find at least one unforgettable fact about the culture and the civilization on your imagined world.

Once you have that framework, filling in the remaining details you will need in order to make that world internally consistent, believable, and fascinating may take some time and some writing—but it should be as much (or more) play than work. My hope is that this tripartite framework liberates you to focus on the play, and that the strategies I've shared in this final chapter will help you invite the reader into that imaginative play without overwhelming or boring them. (Quite the opposite: you want your reader to fall so in love with the imagined world that they crave every bit of information about it they can get.)

I hope that you have enjoyed reading this course-in-a-book as much as I have enjoyed providing it. Do the exercises. Practice. Go get some books on the parts of world design that interest you most—perhaps a book on evolution (to help you design fascinating creatures), or a book on how fishing industries work, or on religions. The more you learn, the more insight you can bring to your writing. I find that any book about culture or law or architecture is infinitely more fascinating if I play the mental game of asking as I read, "How would such and such a society, operating in this way, have dealt with a sudden dragon attack? Would these houses I am reading about have been more or less vulnerable to fire falling from the sky than the house I am living in? How would people with these customs I am reading about have interpreted the sudden rising of the ravenous dead?" (In fact, that's the very kind of imagination game that led to the creation of my *Zombie Bible* novels.)

Research can be pursued endlessly, but I hope this book has offered you a set of provocative questions you can set out to answer, which can provide focus to your creative work. And most of all, I hope you never stop imagining fantastical worlds. That is one thing I have sworn to my nine-year-old self, to that little boy who once roamed the woods behind my father's farm, searching for a crashed spaceship, with a stick in his hand to beat off the schoolbus-sized tarra birds that might swoop low to attack at any moment. I promised him I would never stop imagining extravagant and fascinating worlds. That is a promise worth keeping.

May you make a similar vow, and revel in the fulfillment of it!

STANT LITORE
SEPTEMBER 2017

ACKNOWLEDGMENTS

A BOOK OF THIS KIND doesn't happen without a great deal of help. I'd like to first thank Andrew Hallam, who insisted that the book be written, often and over years. Once I embarked on the project, Andrew's generosity with feedback and insight made it a far better book. Thanks are due to my Patreon members, who fund and encourage my work; to Roberto Calas for his remarkable cover art; to K. Tempest Bradford, Michael Underwood, and M.H. Boroson for kind words about my teaching or about instructional material I provided for writers; and to Richard Ellis Preston, Jr. for offering careful reading and feedback. Also to the many students and writers who asked for the book. I gave in at last and wrote it, and had a wonderful time doing so. To the cast and crew of Pikes Peak Writers Conference, Castle Rock Writers, AnomalyCon, and Myths & Legends Con, who kept inviting me back to teach. And, of course, to all those creators of the fictional worlds that *I* never forget, the ones I don't want to leave. Thank you. Finally but momentously, a thanks to my wife and children, without whose generosity and forbearance neither novels nor courses like this one would exist.

ABOUT THE AUTHOR

Stant Litore writes about zombies, aliens, and tyrannosaurs, and about speculative fiction, religious studies, and sundry other topics. He does not currently own a starship or a time machine but would rather like to. He lives in Aurora, Colorado with his wife and three children and hides from visitors in the basement library beneath a heap of toy dinosaurs, tattered novels, comic books, incomprehensibly scribbled drafts, and antique tomes. He is working on his next novel, or several. You can read some of his current fiction by looking up *Ansible*, *The Running of the Tyrannosaurs*, *The Zombie Bible*, or *Dante's Heart*. However, doing so may have unpredictable effects, and Stant offers no assurances that you will emerge from any of these stories unscathed. Best leave all non-essentials behind, take with you only what you need to survive, and venture into the books cautiously and ready to call for backup. Enjoy, and good luck.

82296973R00102

Made in the USA
Middletown, DE
01 August 2018